Developing Web Services with Apache Axis

Copyright © 2005

Ka Iok 'Kent' Tong

Publisher:	TipTec Development
Author's email:	freemant2000@yahoo.com
Book website:	http://www.agileskills2.org
Notice:	All rights reserved. No part of this publication may be reproduced, stored in a retrieval system or transmitted, in any form or by any means, electronic, mechanical, photocopying, recording, or otherwise, without the prior written permission of the publisher.
Edition:	First edition 2005

Foreword

Learn web services and Apache Axis easily

If you'd like to learn how to create web services (in particular, using Apache Axis) and make some sense of various standards like SOAP, WSDL, JAX-RPC, SOAP with attachments, WS-Security, XML Encryption and XML Signature, then this book is for you. Why?

- It has a tutorial style that walks you through in a step-by-step manner.

- It is concise. There is no lengthy, abstract description.

- Many diagrams are used to show the flow of processing and high level concepts so that you get a whole picture of what's happening.

- The first 40 pages are freely available on http://www.agileskills2.org. You can judge it yourself.

Unique contents in this book

This book covers the following topics not found in other books on Axis:

- How to work with Axis 1.3.

- How to use Eclipse and Tomcat with Axis.

- How to encrypt and sign SOAP messages using WSS4J.

- How to send and receive SOAP attachments.

- How to harden an Axis installation.

Target audience and prerequisites

This book is suitable for those who would like to learn how to develop web services in Java.

In order to understand what's in the book, you need to know Java and to have edited XML files. However, you do NOT need to know the more advanced XML concepts (e.g., XML schema, XML namespace), servlet, Tomcat or PKI.

Acknowledgments

I'd like to thank:

- The Axis developers for creating Axis.
- The WSS4J developers for creating WSS4J.
- Anne Thomas Manes, an expert in web services, for reviewing the book.
- Werner Dittmann, a developer of WSS4J, for reviewing the book.
- Helena Lei for proofreading this book.
- Eugenia Chan Peng U for doing book cover and layout design.

Table of Contents

Foreword...3
   Learn web services and Apache Axis easily.........................3
   Unique contents in this book...3
   Target audience and prerequisites.......................................3
   Acknowledgments..3
Chapter 1 Designing the interface for a simple web service........9
   What's in this chapter?...10
   Providing cross platform operations across the Internet.......10
   RPC style web service..11
   Document style web service..13
   Determining the operation for a document style web service....
   15
   Port type...16
   Binding...17
   Port..18
   Target namespace..20
   WSDL...21
   Summary...22
Chapter 2 Implementing a web service..................................25
   What's in this chapter?...26
   Installing Eclipse...26
   Installing Axis...26
   Installing Tomcat..26
   Setting up the Axis server..28
   Installing WTP..31
   WSDL file for the web service...32
   RPC version of the web service...35
   Using WTP to create the WSDL file....................................36
   Generating service stub...48
   Implementing the web service...51
   Understanding the deployment descriptor...........................53
   Sending the deployment descriptor to the Axis server..........55
   Testing your web service..57
   Creating a client using a generated stub............................58
   Undeploying a web service...61
   Summary...61

Chapter 3 Optimizing the development environment.............63
    What's in this chapter?..64
    Making changes to Java code take effect immediately.........64
    Debugging a web service.......................................67
    Summary..69
Chapter 4 Understanding the calling process...................71
    What's in this chapter?..72
    Calling a web service without a client stub..................72
    Seeing the SOAP messages....................................73
    Letting Axis convert the data...............................77
    Controlling the ordering of the properties..................80
    Summary..80
Chapter 5 Accepting multiple parameters.......................83
    What's in this chapter?..84
    Accepting multiple parameters...............................84
    Creating a DII client to call a wrapped service.............88
    Interoperability..88
    Summary..88
Chapter 6 Sending and receiving complex data structures.......89
    What's in this chapter?..90
    Product query...90
    Sending more data in a message.............................94
    Returning faults..94
    Using encoded..98
    Summary..98
Chapter 7 Sending binary files................................101
    What's in this chapter?..102
    Providing the image of a product...........................102
    Interoperability..105
    Summary..106
Chapter 8 Controlling the life cycle of your back end service
object...107
    What's in this chapter?..108
    A counter web service...108
    Using an application scoped service object..................109
    Using a session scoped service object......................110
    Summary..112
Chapter 9 Signing and encrypting SOAP messages...............113
    What's in this chapter?..114

Private key and public key..114
Digital signature..115
Signing and encrypting...117
Certificate and CA..118
Distinguished name..119
Performance issue with asymmetric encryption..................119
Keeping key pair and certificates in Java..........................120
Generating a key pair...121
Setting up a CA..124
Importing the certificate into the keystore.........................127
Signing a SOAP message...129
Making it optional..135
Using symbolic constants...136
Verifying the digital signature..136
Prompting for the password..138
Performing configurations at deployment time...................139
Letting the DII client use the client-config.wsdd file............142
Retrieving the user information in the back end object.......143
Signing the response message...145
Encrypting the request message...148
Removing dangling references to resources.......................151
Combining signing and encrypting......................................152
Interoperability..155
Summary..156
Chapter 10 Securing an Axis installation..............................159
What's in this chapter?...160
Removing unnecessary servlets..160
Disabling the web service listing...162
Removing the Version web service......................................162
Restricting who can deploy services...................................163
Removing the JWS handler...165
Summary..165
References..167
Alphabetical Index..169

Chapter 1

Designing the interface for a simple web service

What's in this chapter?

In this chapter you'll learn to how to design the interface for a simple web service.

Providing cross platform operations across the Internet

Suppose that you'd like to provide a service to the public or to some business partners: They can send you two strings and you will concatenate them and return the string. Of course, in real world you provide a more useful services.

There are several major requirements: First, the users may be using different languages (Java, C# and etc.) and using different platforms (Windows, Linux and etc.). Your service must be accessible by different languages and platforms. Second, they will call your service across the Internet and there may be firewalls in between. Your service must be able to go through firewalls.

Given these requirements, the best solution is to provide a so called "web service". For example, you may make a web service accessible on the host www.ttdev.com and accessible as /SimpleService (see the diagram below), so the full URL is http://www.ttdev.com/SimpleService. This is called the "endpoint" of the web service. Your web service may support one or more operations. One operation may be named "concat":

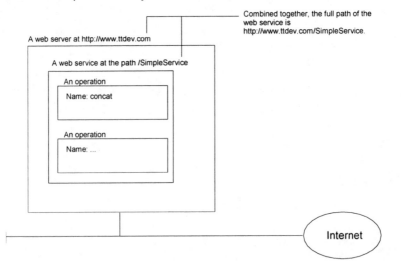

However, you hope to provide a globally unique name to each operation so that you can have your "concat" operation while another person may have his "concat" operation. So, in addition to the name, you may declare that the "concat" name above is in the "namespace" of http://ttdev.com/ss (see the diagram below). A namespace is just like a Java package. But it is not in a dot format like com.ttdev.foo; it is in the format of a URL. So, the full name of the operation will be "concat" in namespace http://ttdev.com/ss. The name "concat" is called the "local name". The full name is called a "QName (qualified name)":

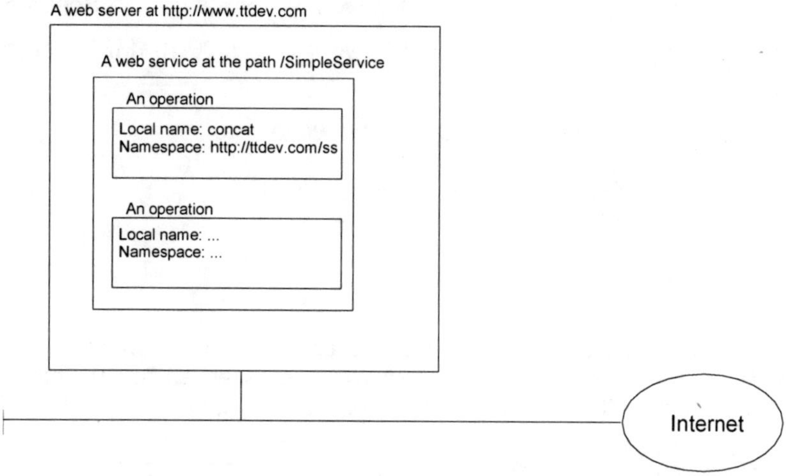

A web server at http://www.ttdev.com

```
A web service at the path /SimpleService

    An operation

    Local name: concat
    Namespace: http://ttdev.com/ss


    An operation

    Local name: ...
    Namespace: ...
```

Internet

You may wonder what this http://ttdev.com/ss namespace means. The answer is that it has no particular meaning. Even though it is a URL, it does NOT mean that you can use a browser to access this URL to get a web page (If you do, you may get a file not found error). The only important thing is that it must be globally unique. As I have registered the domain name ttdev.com, it must be globally unique.

Note that the namespace is a completely different concept from the endpoint. The endpoint really is the location, while the namespace is just a unique id. I could easily move the web service to another web server and thus it will have a different endpoint, but the namespaces of its operations will remain unchanged.

RPC style web service

Your concat operation may take two parameters. One is named "s1" and is a string. The other is named "s2" and is also a string. The return value is also a string:

An operation
```
Local name: concat
Namespace: http://ttdev.com/ss
Parameters:
   s1: string
   s2: string
Return:
   string
```

However, what does the "string" type above mean? Is it the Java string type?

No, you can't say that because it must be language neutral. Fortunately, the XML schema specification defines some basic data types including a string type. Each of these data types has a QName as its id. For example:

Data type	Local name	namespace
string	string	http://www.w3.org/2001/XMLSchema
integer	int	http://www.w3.org/2001/XMLSchema
...	...	...

So, the interface of your operation should be written as:

An operation

```
Local name: concat
Namespace: http://ttdev.com/ss
Parameters:
   s1: string in http://www.w3.org/2001/XMLSchema
   s2: string in http://www.w3.org/2001/XMLSchema
Return:
   string in http://www.w3.org/2001/XMLSchema
```

Actually, in web services, a method call is called an "input message" and a parameter is called a "part". The return value is called an "output message" and may contain multiple parts. So, it is more correct to say:

An operation

```
Local name: concat
Namespace: http://ttdev.com/ss
Input message:
   Part 1:
      Name: s1
      Type: string in http://www.w3.org/2001/XMLSchema
   Part 2:
      Name: s2
      Type: string in http://www.w3.org/2001/XMLSchema
Output message:
   Part 1:
      Name: return
      Type: string in http://www.w3.org/2001/XMLSchema
```

When someone calls this operation, he can send you an XML element as the input message like:

The QName of this XML element is exactly that of the operation he is trying to call

foo is a "namespace prefix" representing the http://ttdev.com/ss in the rest of this element including its children.

```
<foo:concat xmlns:foo="http://ttdev.com/ss">
   <s1>abc</s1>
   <s2>123</s2>
</foo:concat>
```

There is a child element for each part. Each child element has the same name as that part.

When you return, the output message may be like:

```
<foo:output xmlns:foo="http://ttdev.com/ss">
   abc123
</foo:output>
```

This kind of web service is called "RPC style" web service (RPC stands for "Remote Procedure Call"). That is, the operation QName and the names of the parts are used to create the input message.

Document style web service

The above way is not the only way you design the interface of your web service. For example, you may say that its input message only contains a single part (see the diagram below) which is an element defined in a schema. In that schema, it is defined as an element named "concatRequest" that contains two child elements <s1> and <s2>:

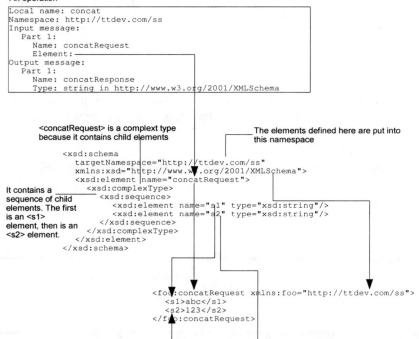

An operation

```
Local name: concat
Namespace: http://ttdev.com/ss
Input message:
   Part 1:
      Name: concatRequest
      Element: ──────
Output message:
   Part 1:
      Name: concatResponse
      Type: string in http://www.w3.org/2001/XMLSchema
```

<concatRequest> is a complex type because it contains child elements

The elements defined here are put into this namespace

```
<xsd:schema
   targetNamespace="http://ttdev.com/ss"
   xmlns:xsd="http://www.w3.org/2001/XMLSchema">
   <xsd:element name="concatRequest">
      <xsd:complexType>
         <xsd:sequence>
            <xsd:element name="s1" type="xsd:string"/>
            <xsd:element name="s2" type="xsd:string"/>
         </xsd:sequence>
      </xsd:complexType>
   </xsd:element>
</xsd:schema>
```

It contains a sequence of child elements. The first is an <s1> element, then is an <s2> element.

```
<foo:concatRequest xmlns:foo="http://ttdev.com/ss">
   <s1>abc</s1>
   <s2>123</s2>
</foo:concatRequest>
```

Note that the schema is included in the interface of your web service:

A web service

A schema

```
<xsd:schema
   targetNamespace="http://ttdev.com/ss"
   xmlns:xsd="http://www.w3.org/2001/XMLSchema">
   <xsd:element name="concatRequest">
     <xsd:complexType>
       <xsd:sequence>
         <xsd:element name="s1" type="xsd:string"/>
         <xsd:element name="s2" type="xsd:string"/>
       </xsd:sequence>
     </xsd:complexType>
   </xsd:element>
</xsd:schema>
```

An operation

```
Local name: concat
Namespace: http://ttdev.com/ss
Input message:
  Part 1:
    Name: concatRequest
    Element: concatRequest in http://ttdev.com/ss
Output message:
  Part 1:
    Name: concatResponse
    Type: string in http://www.w3.org/2001/XMLSchema
```

As you can see above, a part may be declared as a particular element (<concatRequest> defined in your schema) or as any element having a particular type (string defined in XML schema specification). In either case it is identified using a QName.

When someone calls this operation, he will send you a <concatRequest> element as the input message like:

```
<foo:concatRequest xmlns:foo="http://ttdev.com/ss">
  <s1>abc</s1>
  <s2>123</s2>
</foo:concatRequest>
```

When you return, the output message may be like:

Commonly people will use the xsd prefix for it

```
<foo:concatResponse
   xmlns:foo="http://ttdev.com/ss"
   xmlns:xsd="http://www.w3.org/2001/XMLSchema"
   xmlns:xsi="http://www.w3.org/2001/XMLSchema-Instance"
   xsi:type="xsd:string">
   abc123
</foo:concatResponse>
```

This attribute is used to explicitly state the XML element type of the element. This attribute is defined in the http://www.w3.org/2001/XMLSchema-Instance namespace, so you need to introduce a prefix for it:

This kind of web service is called "document style" web service. That is, the input message will contain a single part only which is well defined in a schema.

If you go back to check the input message for the RPC style service, it should be revised as:

```
<foo:concat
  xmlns:foo="http://ttdev.com/ss"
  xmlns:xsd="http://www.w3.org/2001/XMLSchema"
  xmlns:xsi="http://www.w3.org/2001/XMLSchema-Instance">
  <s1 xsi:type="xsd:string">abc</s1>
  <s2 xsi:type="xsd:string">123</s2>
</foo:concat>
```

This is because <foo:concat>, <s1> and <s2> are not defined in any schema and therefore you must explicitly state the XML element types of the content of <s1> and <s2>.

Now, let's compare the input messages of the RPC style web service and the document style web service:

| RPC style | ```<foo:concat
  xmlns:foo="http://ttdev.com/ss"
  xmlns:xsd="http://www.w3.org/2001/XMLSchema"
  xmlns:xsi="http://www.w3.org/2001/XMLSchema-Instance">
  <s1 xsi:type="xsd:string">abc</s1>
  <s2 xsi:type="xsd:string">123</s2>
</foo:concat>``` |
|---|---|
| Document style | ```<foo:concatRequest xmlns:foo="http://ttdev.com/ss">
  <s1>abc</s1>
  <s2>123</s2>
</foo:concatRequest>``` |

Not much difference, right? The significant difference is that the former can't be validated with a schema while the latter can. Therefore, document style web service is becoming the dominant style. According to an organization called "WS-I (web services interoperability organization)", you should use document style web services only.

Determining the operation for a document style web service

To call an operation in a document style web service, one will send the only part of the input message only. Note that it does NOT send the operation name in any way. Then if there are more than one operations in the web service (see the diagram below), how can it determine which one is being called? In that case, it can see if the input message is a <concatRequest> or a <someElement> to determine. What if both take a <someElement>? Then it is an error and it won't work:

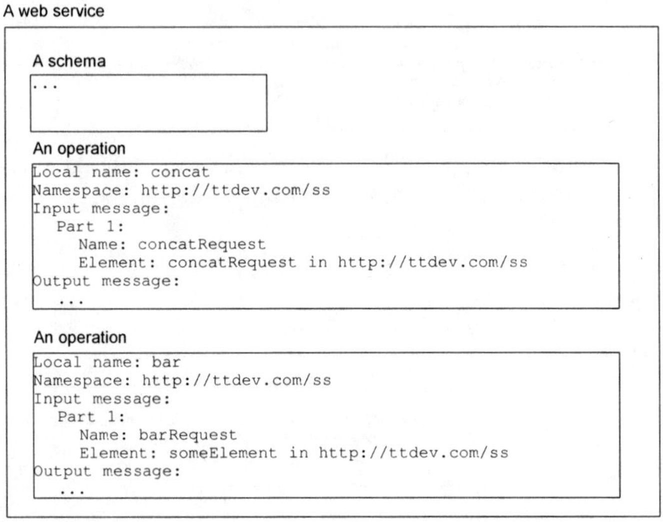

A web service

```
  A schema
  . . .



  An operation
Local name: concat
Namespace: http://ttdev.com/ss
Input message:
   Part 1:
     Name: concatRequest
     Element: concatRequest in http://ttdev.com/ss
Output message:
   . . .

  An operation
Local name: bar
Namespace: http://ttdev.com/ss
Input message:
   Part 1:
     Name: barRequest
     Element: someElement in http://ttdev.com/ss
Output message:
   . . .
```

Port type

Actually, a web service doesn't directly contain a list of operations. Instead (see the diagram below), operations are grouped into one or more "port types". A port type is like a Java class and each operation in it is like a static method. For example, in the web service above, you could have a port type named "stringUtil" containing operations for strings, while having another port type named "dateUtil" containing operations for dates. The name is a port type must also be a QName:

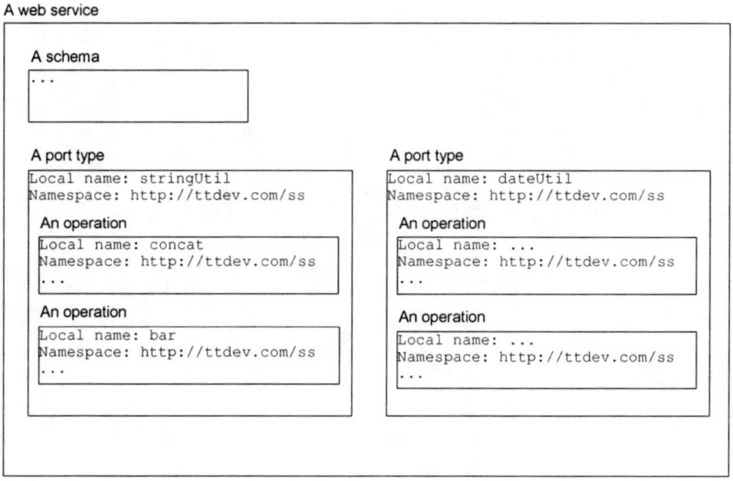

A web service

A schema

. . .

A port type

```
Local name: stringUtil
Namespace: http://ttdev.com/ss
```

An operation

```
Local name: concat
Namespace: http://ttdev.com/ss
...
```

An operation

```
Local name: bar
Namespace: http://ttdev.com/ss
...
```

A port type

```
Local name: dateUtil
Namespace: http://ttdev.com/ss
```

An operation

```
Local name: ...
Namespace: http://ttdev.com/ss
...
```

An operation

```
Local name: ...
Namespace: http://ttdev.com/ss
...
```

Binding

Actually, a port type may allow you to access it using different message formats. The message format that you have seen is called the "Simple Object Access Protocol (SOAP)" format. It is possible that, say, the stringUtil port type may also support a plain text format:

```
concat(s1='abc', s2='123')
```

In addition to the message format, a port type may allow the message to be carried (transported) in an HTTP POST request or in an email. Each supported combination is called a "binding":

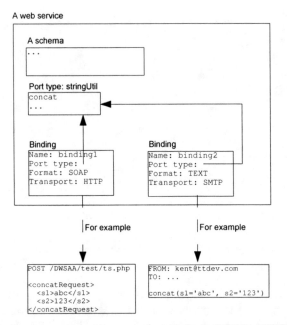

What bindings should your port type support? Only SOAP+HTTP is commonly supported and Axis only supports this combination. So, you probably use this binding only in practice.

Port

Suppose that there are just too many people using your web service, you decide to make it available on more than one computers. For example (see the diagram below), you may deploy the above binding 1 on computers c1, c2 and c3 and deploy binding 2 on c3. In that case it is said that you have four ports. Three ports are using binding 1 and one using binding 2:

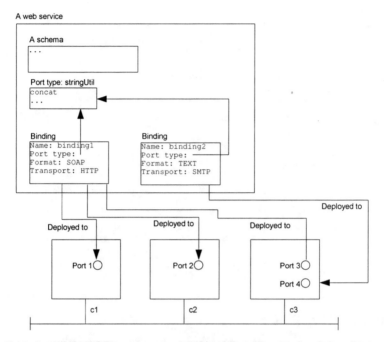

Note that it does NOT mean that the requests received by these three computers will be forwarded to a computer hiding behind for processing. Instead, it means that there is some software implementing the port type installed on these three computers. There is no requirement that the same piece of software is installed onto the different computers. For example, on c1, port 1 may be written in Java, while on c2, port 2 may be written in C#. The important point is that they both support the operations specified in port type stringUtil and the message format and transport specified in the binding 1. Port 4 must also implement the same operations too (same port type) but the message format and transport are different.

To tell others about this arrangement, you include these ports in the interface of the web service:

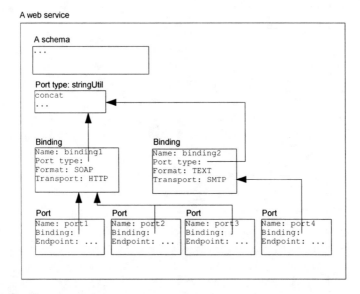

Target namespace

You have been using the same namespace for the operation names, port type names and etc. in this web service. Do they have to be in the same namespace? By default, this is the case: There is a single namespace for a web service to put the names into. This is called the "target namespace" for the web service:

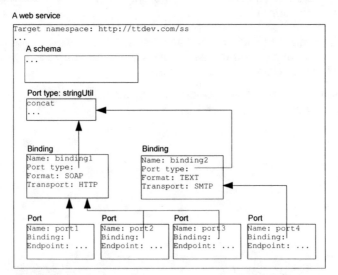

You've been using http://ttdev.com/ss as the target namespace. Is it a good choice? Basically a namespace is good as long as it is globally unique. So this one should be good. However, people may try to download a web page from this URL. When it doesn't work, they may suspect that your web service is out of order. To avoid this confusion, you may use something called URN (Uniform Resource Name) as the namespace.

A namespace must be a URI. URI stands for Uniform Resource Identifier. There are two kinds of URI. One is URL such as http://www.foo.com/bar. The other is URN. A URN takes the format of urn:<some-object-type>:<some-object-id>. For example, International ISBN Agency has made a request to the IANA (International Assigned Numbers Association) that it would like to manage the object type named "isbn". After the request has been approved, the International ISBN Agency can declare that a URN urn:isbn:1-23-456789-0 will identify a book whose ISBN is 1-23-456789-0. It can determine the meaning of the object id without consulting IANA at all.

Similarly, you may submit a request to IANA to register your Internet domain name such as foo.com as the object type. Then on approval you can use URNs like urn:foo.com:xyz identifies an object xyz in your company. What xyz means or its format is completely up to you to decide. For example, you may use urn:foo.com:product:123 (so xyz is product:123) to mean the product #123 produced by your company, or urn:foo.com:patent/123 (so xyz is patent/123) to mean a patent coded 123 in your company.

However, this will create a lot of workload on you and on IANA (one registration per company!). As you have already registered the domain name foo.com, it is unlikely that someone will use it in their URN's. So, you may want to go ahead and use foo.com, or, as many people do, foo-com as the object type without registration with IANA and hope that there won't be any collision.

An XML namespace must be a URI. You can use a URL or a URN. Functionally there is no difference at all. For example, you may use say urn:ttdev.com:ss as the target namespace for your web service instead of http://ttdev.com/ss without changing any functionality.

By the way, if you are going to lookup references on URN, do NOT try to find terms like "object type" or "object id". The official terms are:

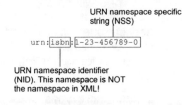

WSDL

By now you have finished designing the interface to your web service:

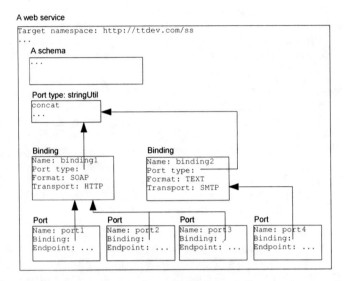

It fully describes your web service. This description language (terms and concepts) is called "WSDL (Web Services Description Language)".

Summary

A web service is platform neutral, language neutral and can be accessed across the Internet.

A web service has one or more ports. Each port is a binding deployed at a certain network address (endpoint). A binding is a port type using a particular message format and a particular transport protocol. A port type contains one or more operations. An operation has an input message and an output message. Each message has one or more parts. Each part is either a certain element defined in the schema of the web service, or any element belonging to a certain element type in that schema. All this information is fully described in WSDL.

To call a RPC style web service, one will create an XML element with the name of the operation and a child element for each of its input message part. To call a document style web service, one will just send the one and only part of its input message. Because the XML element used to call a RPC style web service is not defined in any schema, for better interoperability, one should create document style web services.

The web service, its ports, bindings, port types and operations each has a QName uniquely identifying it. A QName has a local part and an XML namespace. An XML namespace is a URI that is globally unique. By default the names of all these components are put into the target namespace of the web service.

There are two kinds of URI: URL and URN. URN takes the form of urn:<NID>:<NSS>. You can use either as an XML namespace. The only difference is that a URL is suggesting that it is the location of an object, while URN is purely a id of the object.

Chapter 2

Implementing a web service

What's in this chapter?

In this chapter you'll learn to implement the web service interface designed in the previous chapter.

Installing Eclipse

First, you need to make sure you have Eclipse installed. If not, go to http://www.eclipse.org to download the Eclipse platform (e.g., eclipse-platform-3.1-win32.zip) and the Eclipse Java Development Tool (eclipse-JDT-3.1.zip). Unzip both into c:\eclipse. Then, create a shortcut to run "c:\eclipse\eclipse -data c:\workspace". This way, it will store your projects under the c:\workspace folder. To see if it's working, run it and then you should be able to switch to the Java perspective:

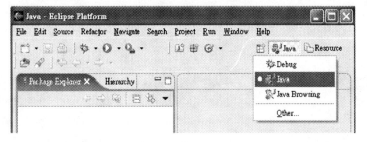

Installing Axis

Next, go to http://ws.apache.org/axis to download a binary package of Axis (e.g., axis-bin-1_3.zip). Unzip it into a folder say c:\axis.

Axis uses the JavaMail API, you need to download it from http://java.sun.com/products/javamail/downloads/index.html. Suppose that it is javamail-1_3_3_01.zip. Unzip it into say c:\javamail.

Axis also uses the JavaBeans Activation Framework. You can download it from http://java.sun.com/products/javabeans/glasgow/jaf.html. Suppose that it is jaf-1_0_2-upd2.zip. Unzip it into say c:\jaf.

Installing Tomcat

First, you need to install Tomcat. Go to http://jakarta.apache.org to download a binary package of Tomcat. Download the zip version (do NOT download the Windows exe version). Suppose that it is jakarta-tomcat-5.5.7.zip. Unzip it into a folder (suppose that it is c:\tomcat). If you're going to use Tomcat 5.5 with JDK 1.4 or 1.3, you also need to download the compat package and unzip it into c:\tomcat.

Before you can run it, make sure the environment variable JAVA_HOME is defined to point to your JDK folder (e.g., C:\Program Files\Java\jdk1.5.0_02):

If you don't have it, define it now. Now, open a command prompt, change to c:\tomcat\bin and then run startup.bat. If it is working, you should see:

Open a browser and go to http://localhost:8080 and you should see:

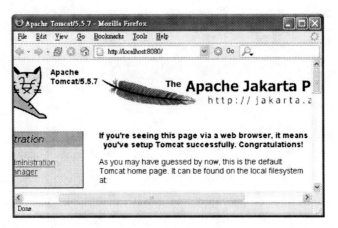

Let's shut it down by changing to c:\tomcat\bin and running shutdown.bat.

Setting up the Axis server

The Axis server is in c:\axis\webapps\axis (assuming you have installed Axis into c:\axis). In addition, it needs access to the JavaMail API and JavaBeans Activation Framework. So,   copy c:\javamail\mail.jar and c:\jaf\activation.jar into c:\axis\webapps\axis\WEB-INF\lib:

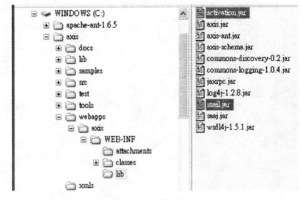

If you're using Tomcat 4.x and JDK 1.4, you need to copy jaxrpc.jar and saaj.jar in c:\axis\webapps\axis\WEB-INF\lib into c:\tomcat\common\lib. This is because these jar files contain some classes in the java.* or javax.* packages. In order to prevent some random Jack and Joe from replacing system classes, Tomcat will NOT load such jar files unless they are placed into an "official library folder" such as c:\tomcat\common\lib.

Next, you need to register the Axis server with Tomcat. To do that, create a file Axis.xml in c:\tomcat\conf\Catalina\localhost:

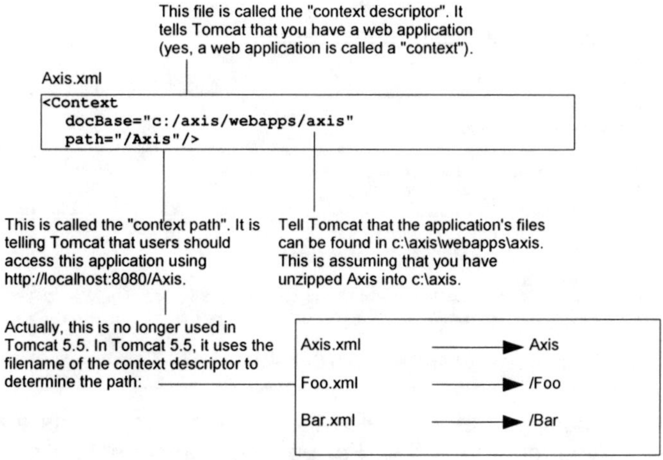

This file is called the "context descriptor". It tells Tomcat that you have a web application (yes, a web application is called a "context").

Axis.xml

```
<Context
    docBase="c:/axis/webapps/axis"
    path="/Axis"/>
```

This is called the "context path". It is telling Tomcat that users should access this application using http://localhost:8080/Axis.

Tell Tomcat that the application's files can be found in c:\axis\webapps\axis. This is assuming that you have unzipped Axis into c:\axis.

Actually, this is no longer used in Tomcat 5.5. In Tomcat 5.5, it uses the filename of the context descriptor to determine the path:

Axis.xml	——————▶ Axis
Foo.xml	——————▶ /Foo
Bar.xml	——————▶ /Bar

Now, start Tomcat (by running startup.bat). To run the Axis server, open a browser and try to go to http://localhost:8080/Axis. You should see:

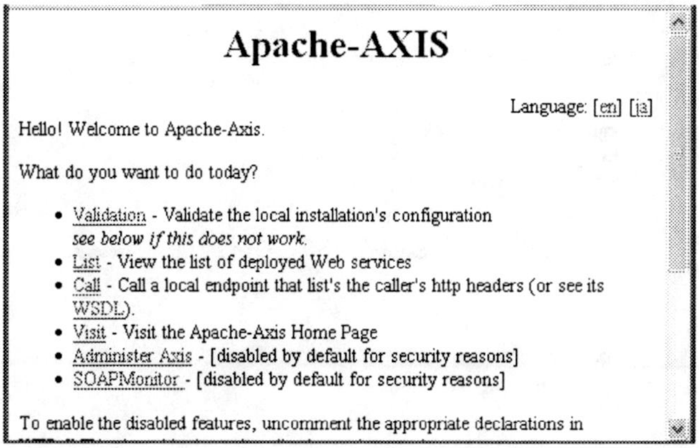

Apache-AXIS

Language: [en] [ja]

Hello! Welcome to Apache-Axis.

What do you want to do today?

- Validation - Validate the local installation's configuration *see below if this does not work.*
- List - View the list of deployed Web services
- Call - Call a local endpoint that list's the caller's http headers (or see its WSDL).
- Visit - Visit the Apache-Axis Home Page
- Administer Axis - [disabled by default for security reasons]
- SOAPMonitor - [disabled by default for security reasons]

To enable the disabled features, uncomment the appropriate declarations in

To further check if it's working, click on the "Validation" link. If it's working, you should see:

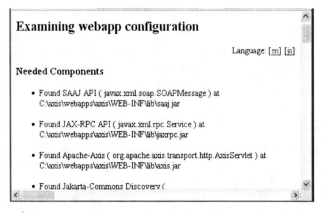

Scroll down the page to make sure all the needed components are found. If any is missing, you must fix it first. For optional components, it's OK to miss any of them:

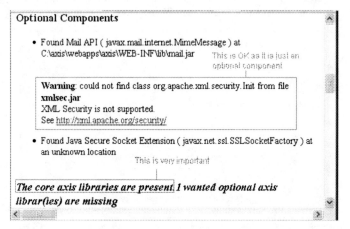

To be absolutely sure that it's working, click the "Call" link below. This will call a sample web service in the Axis server:

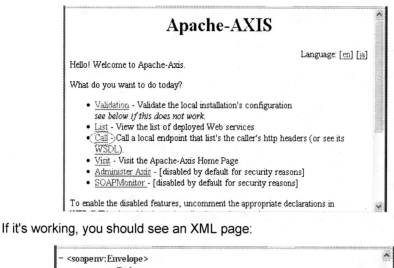

If it's working, you should see an XML page:

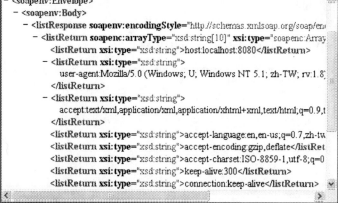

Installing WTP

Next, you need to install the Eclipse WTP (web tools platform). Choose "Help | Software Updates | Find and Install", choose "Search for new features to install", choose "Eclipse.org update site", choose the main site. If you see "WTP" available for install, choose it and then click "Select Required". Otherwise, choose EMF, GEF, JEM:

Then complete the installation. Next, go to http://download.eclipse.org/webtools/downloads to download WTP. Suppose that it is wtp-1.0.zip. Shutdown Eclipse, unzip that zip file into c:\eclipse and restart Eclipse (You may need to specify the -clean option to tell Eclipse to re-scan all the plugins).

WSDL file for the web service

Suppose that you'd like to create a web service described in the previous chapter:

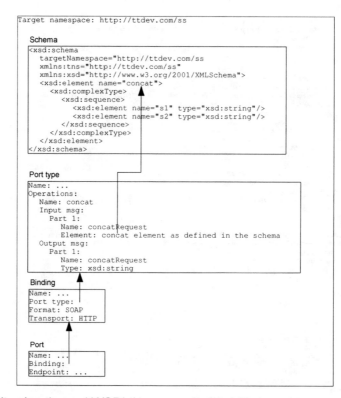

To write it using the real WSDL language, it should be:

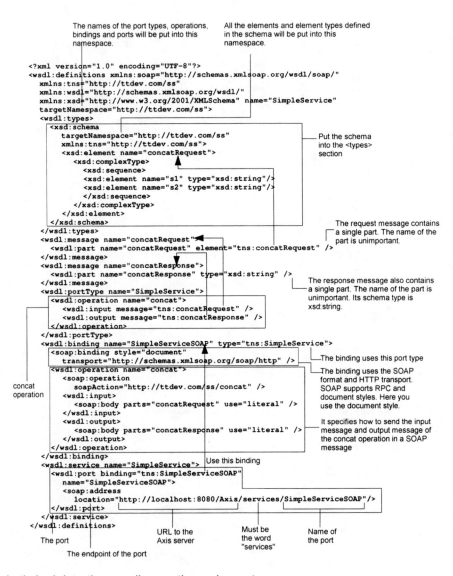

The names of the port types, operations, bindings and ports will be put into this namespace.

All the elements and element types defined in the schema will be put into this namespace.

```xml
<?xml version="1.0" encoding="UTF-8"?>
<wsdl:definitions xmlns:soap="http://schemas.xmlsoap.org/wsdl/soap/"
  xmlns:tns="http://ttdev.com/ss"
  xmlns:wsdl="http://schemas.xmlsoap.org/wsdl/"
  xmlns:xsd="http://www.w3.org/2001/XMLSchema" name="SimpleService"
  targetNamespace="http://ttdev.com/ss">
  <wsdl:types>
    <xsd:schema
      targetNamespace="http://ttdev.com/ss"
      xmlns:tns="http://ttdev.com/ss">
      <xsd:element name="concatRequest">
        <xsd:complexType>
          <xsd:sequence>
            <xsd:element name="s1" type="xsd:string"/>
            <xsd:element name="s2" type="xsd:string"/>
          </xsd:sequence>
        </xsd:complexType>
      </xsd:element>
    </xsd:schema>
  </wsdl:types>
  <wsdl:message name="concatRequest">
    <wsdl:part name="concatRequest" element="tns:concatRequest" />
  </wsdl:message>
  <wsdl:message name="concatResponse">
    <wsdl:part name="concatResponse" type="xsd:string" />
  </wsdl:message>
  <wsdl:portType name="SimpleService">
    <wsdl:operation name="concat">
      <wsdl:input message="tns:concatRequest" />
      <wsdl:output message="tns:concatResponse" />
    </wsdl:operation>
  </wsdl:portType>
  <wsdl:binding name="SimpleServiceSOAP" type="tns:SimpleService">
    <soap:binding style="document"
      transport="http://schemas.xmlsoap.org/soap/http" />
    <wsdl:operation name="concat">
      <soap:operation
        soapAction="http://ttdev.com/ss/concat" />
      <wsdl:input>
        <soap:body parts="concatRequest" use="literal" />
      </wsdl:input>
      <wsdl:output>
        <soap:body parts="concatResponse" use="literal" />
      </wsdl:output>
    </wsdl:operation>
  </wsdl:binding>
  <wsdl:service name="SimpleService">
    <wsdl:port binding="tns:SimpleServiceSOAP"
      name="SimpleServiceSOAP">
      <soap:address
        location="http://localhost:8080/Axis/services/SimpleServiceSOAP"/>
    </wsdl:port>
  </wsdl:service>
</wsdl:definitions>
```

Put the schema into the <types> section

The request message contains a single part. The name of the part is unimportant.

The response message also contains a single part. The name of the part is unimportant. Its schema type is xsd:string.

concat operation

The binding uses this port type

The binding uses the SOAP format and HTTP transport. SOAP supports RPC and document styles. Here you use the document style.

It specifies how to send the input message and output message of the concat operation in a SOAP message

Use this binding

The port

The endpoint of the port

URL to the Axis server

Must be the word "services"

Name of the port

Let's look into the <wsdl:operation> element:

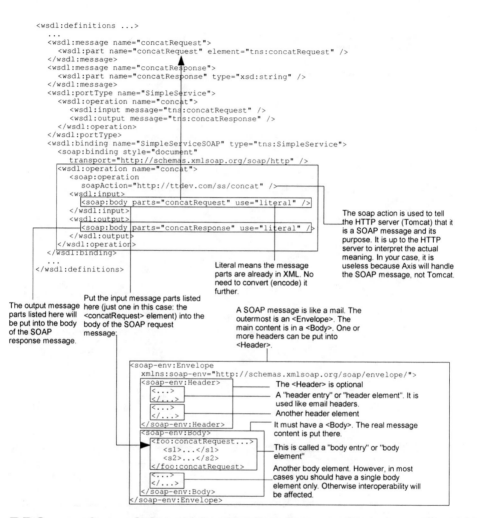

The soap action is used to tell the HTTP server (Tomcat) that it is a SOAP message and its purpose. It is up to the HTTP server to interpret the actual meaning. In your case, it is useless because Axis will handle the SOAP message, not Tomcat.

Literal means the message parts are already in XML. No need to convert (encode) it further.

The output message parts listed here will be put into the body of the SOAP response message.

Put the input message parts listed here (just one in this case: the <concatRequest> element) into the body of the SOAP request message;

A SOAP message is like a mail. The outermost is an <Envelope>. The main content is in a <Body>. One or more headers can be put into <Header>.

The <Header> is optional

A "header entry" or "header element". It is used like email headers.

Another header element

It must have a <Body>. The real message content is put there.

This is called a "body entry" or "body element"

Another body element. However, in most cases you should have a single body element. Otherwise interoperability will be affected.

RPC version of the web service

If the web service was a RPC style service, then the WSDL file would be like:

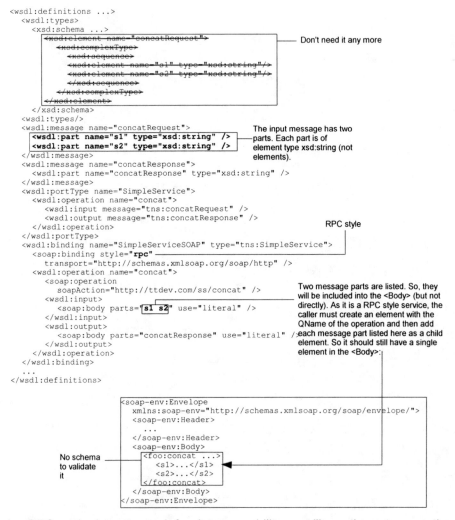

As RPC style is not good for interoperability, you'll continue to use the document style version.

Using WTP to create the WSDL file

It may be error prone to hand create such a WSDL file. Instead, you may use the WTP to do it. First, create a new Java project named SimpleService in Eclipse:

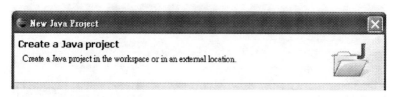

Then, choose the "Libraries" tab:

Click "Add Library" and choose "User Library":

Click "Next":

Click "User Libraries" to define your library containing the jar files in Axis:

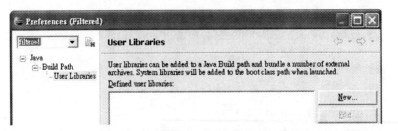

Click "New" to define a new one and enter "Axis" as the name of the library:

Click "Add JARs", browse to c:\axis\webapps\axis\WEB-INF\lib and add all the jar files there:

Then go ahead and complete the creation of the project. Next, right click the project and choose "New | Other" and then "XML | WSDL":

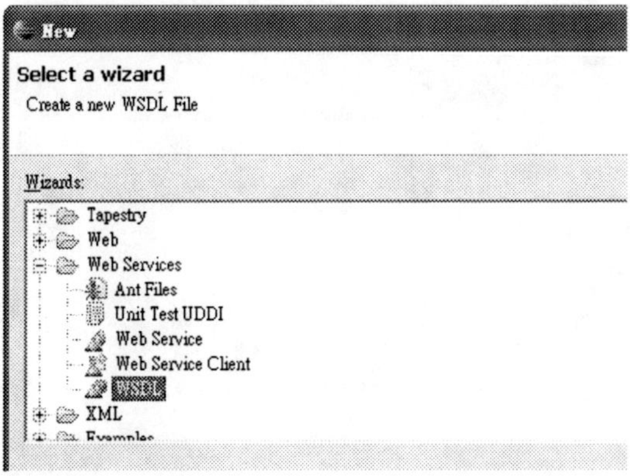

If you don't see this option, it means you haven't installed WTP successfully. If it is working, click "Next" and enter SimpleService.wsdl as the filename:

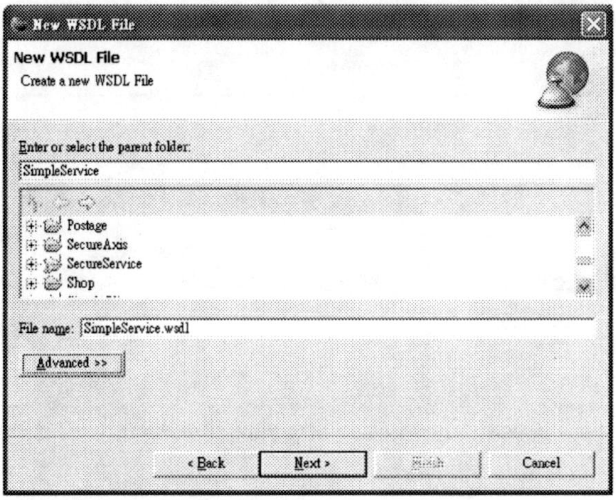

Click "Next". Then input as shown below:

Click "Finish". Then you will something like:

Expand the SimpleService port type and choose operation named "NewOperation", then enter "concat" as the new name:

Then expand the concat operation and choose its input. You should see an arrow connecting it to the concatRequest message:

Expand the concatRequest message and you will find that it contains a single part only with the same name ("concatRequest"):

Note it is a <concatRequest> element that is an xsd:string. This is not what you want. You'd like it to be a <concatRequest> element that contains <s1> and <s2>. So, you need to edit the schema:

This is the target namespace of the
schema. Here it is used to represent
the schema.

Definition			
Imports		Types	
		⇨ S http://ttdev.com/ss	

Services	Bindings	Port Types	Messages

⊞ SimpleService	⊞ SimpleServiceSOAP	⊟ SimpleService
		  ⊟ concat
		    input
		    output
			⊟ concatRequest
			  concatRequest (ms:concatRequest)
			⊞ concatResponse

Double click on the schema. This will open the schema for editing:

Schema : http://ttdev.com/ss	
Directives	
Elements	Types
e concatRequest e concatResponse	

To edit the <concatRequest>, double click on it. Then you will see:

concatRequest
type = xsd:string

Right click it and choose "Set Type | New Complex Type":

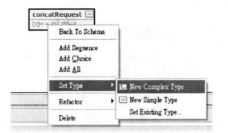

concatRequest
type = xsd:string
    Back To Schema

    Add Sequence
    Add Choice
    Add All

    Set Type   ▶ New Complex Type
    Refactor   ▶ New Simple Type
    Delete   Set Existing Type...

Then you will see that a <sequence> has been added to its content
automatically:

A sequence

concatRequest
type = ...   [⊟]━━[⋯]

Right click the sequence and choose "Add Element":

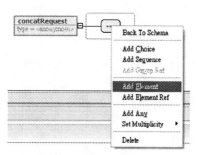

Choose that element and set its name to "s1" and its type to xsd:string (actually xsd:string is the default):

Schema : http://ttdev.com/ss

Directives

Elements
- concatRequest
- concatResponse

Types

Similarly, add another child element <s2> after <s1>. The result should be like:

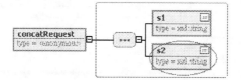

Go back to the schema by clicking the back arrow:

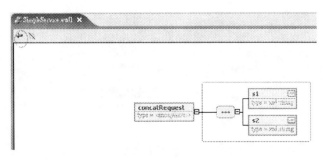

Now the schema is like:

You don't need the <concatResponse> element because it should be just an xsd:string. So, right click it and choose "Delete". Then the schema will be like:

Go back to the WSDL file by choosing the back arrow again. Choose the single part in the input message and make sure it is ultimately connected to the <concatRequest> element:

To double check the input message is indeed using the right schema element, choose the sinlge message part in the concatRequest message, you should see:

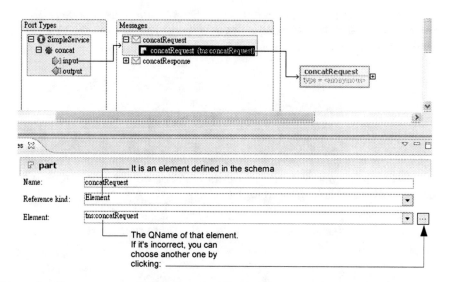

Now, for the response message, it will contain a single part that is just an xsd:string. So, choose that single part and set its properties as shown below:

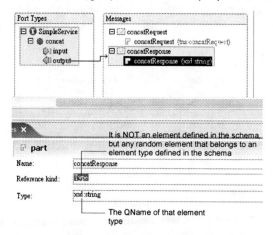

Now the port type, messages and schema are done. The next step is the binding. Choose the operation named "NewOperation" in the existing SimpleServiceSOAP binding:

It must correspond to the concat operation. So, rename it as "concat". Choose something else and then choose it again will show an arrow linking it to the concat operation:

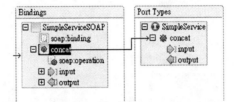

This is what you want. If you choose its input or output, you should see a sequence of arrows linking them together:

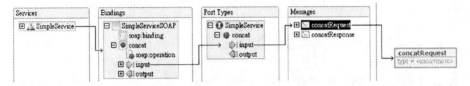

It is critical that they are indeed connected. Expand the input of the binding and choose the <soap:body> element, it specifies which parts to include in the body of the SOAP message. You should set it to the one and only part in the input message:

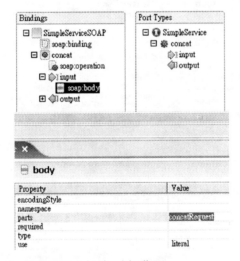

Do the same thing for the output in the binding:

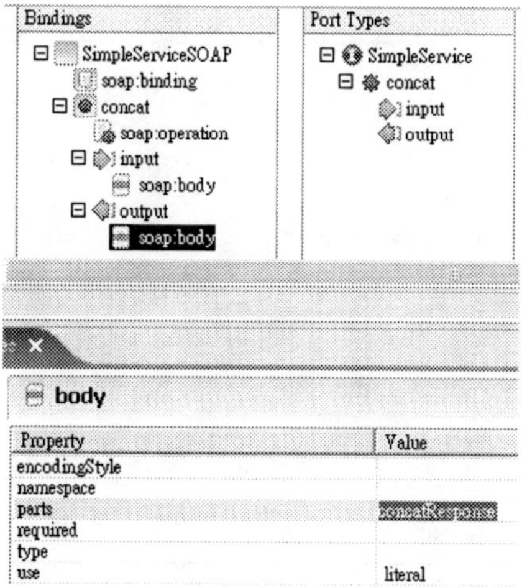

Bindings

- SimpleServiceSOAP
  - soap:binding
  - concat
    - soap:operation
    - input
      - soap:body
    - output
      - soap:body

Port Types

- SimpleService
  - concat
    - input
    - output

body

Property	Value
encodingStyle	
namespace	
parts	concatResponse
required	
type	
use	literal

Next, set the endpoint:

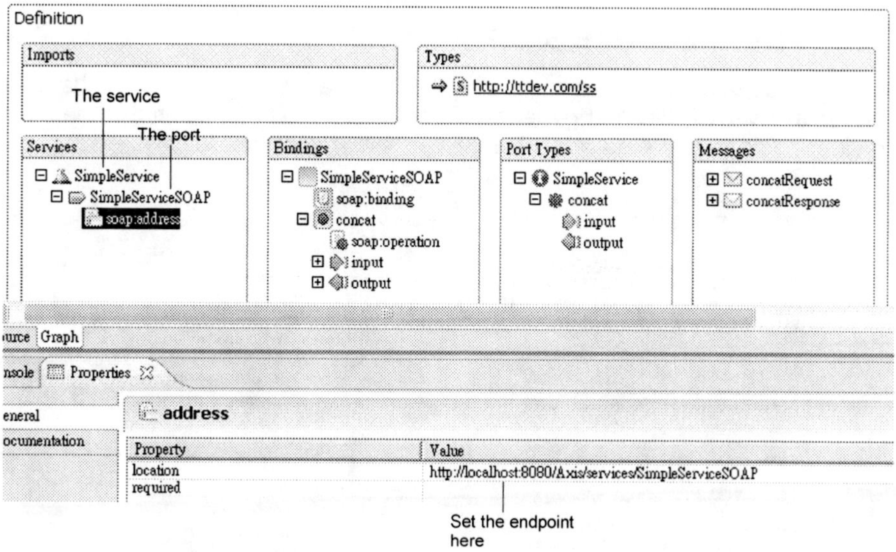

Definition

Imports

The service

The port

Types

⇒ http://ttdev.com/ss

Services

- SimpleService
  - SimpleServiceSOAP
    - soap:address

Bindings

- SimpleServiceSOAP
  - soap:binding
  - concat
    - soap:operation
    - input
    - output

Port Types

- SimpleService
  - concat
    - input
    - output

Messages

- concatRequest
- concatResponse

Source Graph

Console Properties

General

Documentation

address

Property	Value
location	http://localhost:8080/Axis/services/SimpleServiceSOAP
required	

Set the endpoint
here

Now, save the file. If you'd like to see its source, choose the "Source" tab:

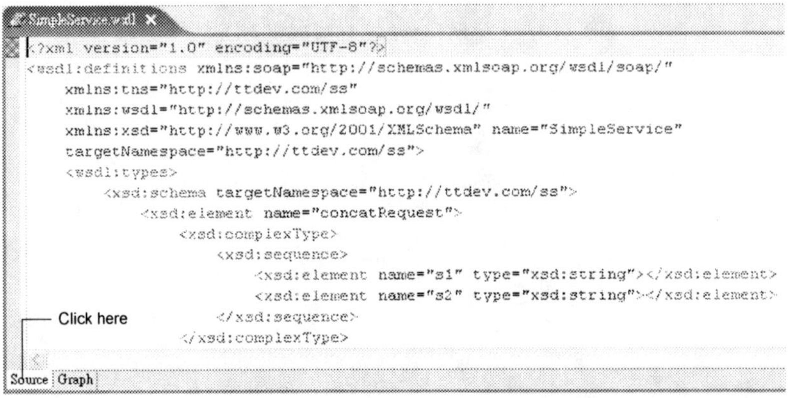

```
SimpleService.wsdl ✕
<?xml version="1.0" encoding="UTF-8"?>
<wsdl:definitions xmlns:soap="http://schemas.xmlsoap.org/wsdl/soap/"
    xmlns:tns="http://ttdev.com/ss"
    xmlns:wsdl="http://schemas.xmlsoap.org/wsdl/"
    xmlns:xsd="http://www.w3.org/2001/XMLSchema" name="SimpleService"
    targetNamespace="http://ttdev.com/ss">
    <wsdl:types>
        <xsd:schema targetNamespace="http://ttdev.com/ss">
            <xsd:element name="concatRequest">
                <xsd:complexType>
                    <xsd:sequence>
                        <xsd:element name="s1" type="xsd:string"></xsd:element>
                        <xsd:element name="s2" type="xsd:string"></xsd:element>
                    </xsd:sequence>
                </xsd:complexType>
```

Click here

Source Graph

To see the GUI editor again, just click the "Graph" tab. Now you're done. Of course, if you don't like using the GUI editor, you can just open using a text editor and input the text directly.

Generating service stub

Now, you can run a program called WSDL2Java coming with Axis that will inspect this WSDL file and generate some basic code to implement the web service. To do that, create a build.xml file in the project root folder:

A project contains one or more "targets". A target is just a job to do.

Set some properties. Here they are the paths to Axis, JavaMail and JavaBeans Activation Framework.

```
<project name="SimpleService">
    <property name="axis.home" value="c:/axis"/>
    <property name="javamail.home" value="c:/javamail-1.3.3_01"/>
    <property name="jaf.home" value="c:/jaf-1.0.2"/>
    <path id="axis.classpath">
        <fileset dir="${axis.home}/lib">
            <include name="**/*.jar" />
        </fileset>
        <fileset dir="${javamail.home}">
            <include name="**/*.jar" />
        </fileset>
        <fileset dir="${jaf.home}">
            <include name="**/*.jar" />
        </fileset>
    </path>
    <taskdef
        resource="axis-tasks.properties"
        classpathref="axis.classpath" />
    <target name="generate-service-stub">
        <axis-wsdl2java
            serverside="true"
            url="SimpleService.wsdl">
        </axis-wsdl2java>
    </target>
</project>
```

A <path> represents a set of paths

Look for files in c:/axis/lib. ${axis.home} is replaced by the value of the axis.home property (c:/axis).

This will match even sub-folders. So, this will include all *.jar files under c:/axis/lib including sub-folders.

Include all *.jar files under c:/javamail-1.3.3_01

Include all *.jar files under c:/jaf-1.0.2

Look for a <path> with this id. Then for each jar file there, try to load a file axis-tasks.properties. This file is provided by Axis that defines some tasks for you to call.

Set this to true. Otherwise it will generate basic code for the client.

The path to the WSDL file. Here you are using a relative path. It is relative to the build.xml file (project root).

One of those tasks defined by Axis is called "axis-wsdl2java". It can generate basic code for the service given a WSDL file.

To run this file, right click it and then choose "Run As | Ant Build..." as shown below:

Then choose the target and click "Run":

You should see that it is working in the console:

```
Console  X    Properties
<terminated> SimpleService build.xml [Ant Build] C:\Program Files\Java\jre1.5.0_02\bin\javaw.exe (Dec 31, 2005 11:06:04 A
Buildfile: C:\workspace\SimpleService\build.xml
generate-service-stub:
[axis-wsdl2java] WSDL2Java C:\workspace\SimpleService\SimpleService.wsdl
BUILD SUCCESSFUL
Total time: 6 seconds
```

Then refresh the project and you'll see that some Java files have been created:

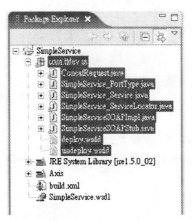

Note that these files have been put into the package com.ttdev.ss. Why? Because the names of the port type, the port and the web service are all in the namespace http://ttdev.com/ss, WSDL2Java simply converts the namespace to a Java package using the following method:

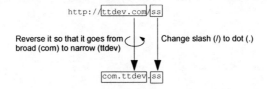

If you don't like it to map namespace http://ttdev.com/ss to package com.ttdev.ss, instead, you would like to map it to com.ttdev.simpleservice, you can do it this way:

```
<project name="SimpleService">
    ...
  <target name="generate-service-stub">
    <axis-wsdl2java
      serverside="true"
      url="SimpleService.wsdl">
      <mapping
        namespace="http://ttdev.com/ss"
        package="com.ttdev.simpleservice"/>
    </axis-wsdl2java>
  </target>
</project>
```

Now, delete the package com.ttdev.ss (including the files in it). Then run the build file again. Refresh the project and you'll see that the files have been put into the com.ttdev.simpleservice package:

Implementing the web service

To implement the web serivce, modify the SimpleServiceSOAPImpl.java file:

```
public class SimpleServiceSOAPImpl implements SimpleService_PortType{
  public String concat(ConcatRequest concatRequest)
    throws java.rmi.RemoteException {
    return concatRequest.getS1()+concatRequest.getS2();
  }
}
```

The ConcatRequest is Java class WSDL2Java created for you. It represents the single message part (the <concatRequest> element).

Eclipse will automatically compile your Java files and generate the corresponding class files in the c:\workspace\SimpleService\com\ttdev\simpleservice folder:

You need to make the classes above available to the Axis server. So copy the whole package folder tree into the Axis server as shown below:

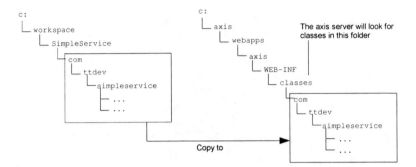

However, as the Axis server is already running, it won't notice the new class files put there. To solve this problem, you can either restart Tomcat (which will restart all web applications in it including the Axis server) or restart just the Axis server. How to do the latter? To do that, go to http://localhost:8080 and choose "Tomcat Manager", but it requires you to enter a user name and password:

Therefore, you need to create a user account first. To do that, edit c:\tomcat\conf\tomcat-users.xml:

```xml
<?xml version='1.0' encoding='utf-8'?>
<tomcat-users>
  <role rolename="tomcat"/>
  <role rolename="role1"/>
  <role rolename="manager"/>
  <user username="tomcat" password="tomcat" roles="tomcat"/>
  <user username="role1" password="tomcat" roles="role1"/>
  <user username="both" password="tomcat" roles="tomcat,role1"/>
  <user username="tomcatAdmin" password="123456" roles="manager"/>
</tomcat-users>
```

Then, restart Tomcat so that it can see the user account. Then, using this account to access the Tomcat Manager:

Path	Display Name	Running	Sessions	Commands
/	Welcome to Tomcat	true	0	Start Stop Reload Undeploy
/Album	Album	true	0	Start Stop Reload Undeploy
/Axis	Apache-Axis	true	0	Start Stop Reload Undeploy
/Bank	Bank	true	0	Start Stop Reload Undeploy
/ComponentUser	ComponentUser	true	0	Start Stop Reload Undeploy
/Components	Components	true	0	Start Stop Reload Undeploy
/ConfirmDelete	ConfirmDelete	true	0	Start Stop Reload Undeploy
/CurrentDate	CurrentDate	true	0	Start Stop Reload Undeploy

To restart the Axis server, just click "Reload" for /Axis. However, as you have already restarted Tomcat, all the applications have been reloaded in the process.

Understanding the deployment descriptor

Having the Java class available to the Axis server isn't enough. You must tell it to create a web service from that class. To do that, use the deploy.wsdd file generated by WSDL2Java. WSDD stands for Web Service Deployment Descriptor. Open it in Eclipse:

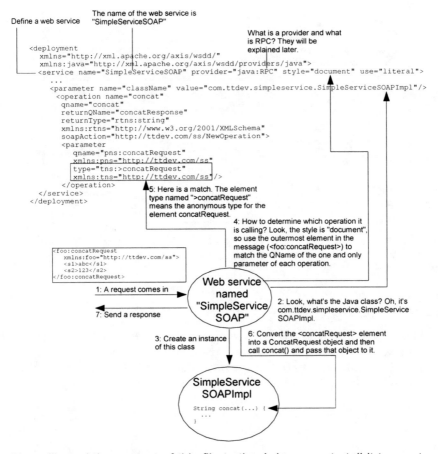

You will send the content of this file to the Axis server to tell it to create your web service. The elements used in the file such as <deployment> and <service> are defined by Axis in the namespace http://xml.apache.org/axis/wsdd/.

So, what's a provider and what is that java:RPC? When you call a web service, a provider is the object that first receives the request. Then it needs to decide how to handle the request. There are several types of providers provided by Axis and each type works differently. Each type of provider has a QName as its unique identifier. In the deployment descriptor you specify the QName of the type of provider you'd like to use:

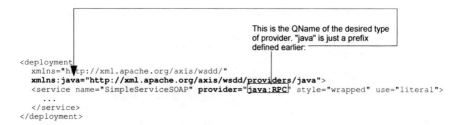

```
<deployment
   xmlns="http://xml.apache.org/axis/wsdd/"
   xmlns:java="http://xml.apache.org/axis/wsdd/providers/java">
   <service name="SimpleServiceSOAP" provider="java:RPC" style="wrapped" use="literal">
      ...
   </service>
</deployment>
```

So, in this case, you're using the type of provider named "RPC" in the namespace http://xml.apache.org/axis/wsdd/providers/java. Note that it is NOT the same RPC as in RPC style vs. document style. No matter your web service is RPC style or document style, you will typically use this type of provider. As you have seen, this type of provider will call create Java object from the class you specified to handle the request, before it sends a response to the client:

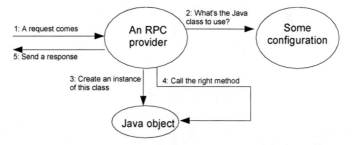

Sending the deployment descriptor to the Axis server

Finally, you need to send the deploy.wsdd file to the Axis server. To do that, edit build.xml:

The URL of the Axis server. This axis-admin task will send an HTTP request to it. More accurately, it will send the HTTP request to the Axis "servlet" in it. What's a servlet? A servlet is a Java object that can handle HTTP requests.

A new target named "deploy"

```
<project name="SimpleService">
   ...
   <target name="generate-service-stub">
      ...
   </target>
   <target name="deploy">
      <axis-admin
         url="http://localhost:8080/Axis/servlet/AxisServlet"
         xmlfile="com/ttdev/simpleservice/deploy.wsdd"/>
   </target>
</project>
```

The path to the Axis servlet

The path to the WSDD file on your computer. It can be an absolutely path or a relative path. If the latter, it is relative to the current folder (the folder containing build.xml, i.e., the project root).

Now, right click the build.xml file and choose "Run As | Ant Build...":

Choose the "deploy" target:

Run it and you should see something like this in the console:

It means you have deployed the web service successfully. If you check the c:\axis\webapps\axis\WEB-INF folder, you will see that a file server-config.wsdd has just been created:

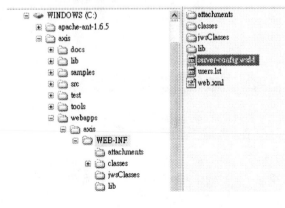

This file is an XML file that contains the configuration of the Axis server, including all the deployed web services. Its content is like:

```xml
<?xml version="1.0" encoding="UTF-8"?>
<deployment
  xmlns="http://xml.apache.org/axis/wsdd/"
  xmlns:java="http://xml.apache.org/axis/wsdd/providers/java">
  ...
  <handler name="LocalResponder"
    type="java:org.apache.axis.transport.local.LocalResponder"/>
  <handler name="URLMapper"
    type="java:org.apache.axis.handlers.http.URLMapper"/>
  <handler name="Authenticate"
    type="java:org.apache.axis.handlers.SimpleAuthenticationHandler"/>
  <service name="AdminService" provider="java:MSG">
    <parameter name="allowedMethods" value="AdminService"/>
    <parameter name="enableRemoteAdmin" value="false"/>
    <parameter name="className" value="org.apache.axis.utils.Admin"/>
    <namespace>http://xml.apache.org/axis/wsdd/</namespace>
  </service>
  <service name="SimpleServiceSOAP" provider="java:RPC" ...>
    <parameter name="..." value="..."/>
    ...
  </service>
  <service name="Version" provider="java:RPC">
    <parameter name="allowedMethods" value="getVersion"/>
    <parameter name="className" value="org.apache.axis.Version"/>
  </service>
  ...
</deployment>
```

Note that it is also a WSDD file just like your deploy.wsdd. Whenever the Axis server is started, it will load this file automatically. It means your web service will remain there even the Axis server is restarted.

Testing your web service

To see if your web service is working, go to http://localhost:8080/Axis again:

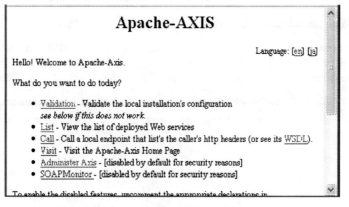

Click "List" to see all the deployed web services:

Note that your SimpleServiceSOAP should be listed there. To see its WSDL file, just click the "wsdl" link:

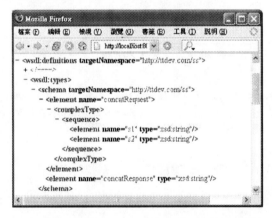

Creating a client using a generated stub

To call this web service, you can ask WSDL2Java to generate a "client stub". When you call a method on it (see the diagram below), it will convert your Java data/objects into the right format (XML), create a request message in the right format (SOAP), send it over the Internet to the right endpoint using the right transport protocol (HTTP) to invoke that operation, wait for the response message, convert the XML back into Java data/object and then return it to you:

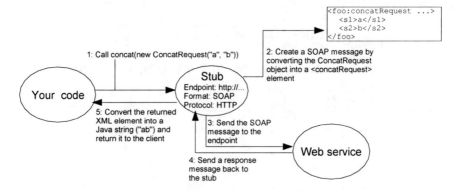

To implement this idea, add another target to build.xml:

```
<project name="SimpleService">
  ...
  <target name="generate-service-stub">
    <axis-wsdl2java
      serverside="true"
      url="SimpleService.wsdl">
      <mapping
        namespace="http://ttdev.com/ss"
        package="com.ttdev.simpleservice"/>
    </axis-wsdl2java>
  </target>
  <target name="generate-client-stub">
    <axis-wsdl2java
      url="SimpleService.wsdl">
      <mapping
        namespace="http://ttdev.com/ss"
        package="com.ttdev.simpleservice.client"/>
    </axis-wsdl2java>
  </target>
  ...
</project>
```

Everything is the same as for generating service stub except the serverside option is not set and that you're putting the code into a sub-package "client". Note that you're using the original SimpleService.wsdl file created by you instead of the one generated by Axis. This is better as you're sure it must be correct. Now, run the target to generate the client stub. You'll see some files are generated:

SimpleService_PortType is the interface representing the port type:

```
public interface SimpleService_PortType extends java.rmi.Remote {
   public String concat(ConcatRequest concatRequest)
      throws java.rmi.RemoteException;
}
```

ConcatRequest is a class representing the <concatRequest> element:

```
public class ConcatRequest  implements java.io.Serializable {
   private java.lang.String s1;
   private java.lang.String s2;

   public ConcatRequest(java.lang.String s1, java.lang.String s2) {
      this.s1 = s1;
      this.s2 = s2;
   }
   . . .
}
```

SimpleServiceSOAPStub is a class representing the (SOAP+HTTP) binding:

```
public class SimpleServiceSOAPStub extends org.apache.axis.client.Stub
   implements SimpleService_PortType {
   public String concat(ConcatRequest concatRequest)
      throws java.rmi.RemoteException {
      . . .
   }
   . . .
}
```

Note that it implements the port type interface. It has hard coded the message format and transport protocol in its source code. That's why this class is a concrete class while the port type is an interface. It also has a field for the endpoint that you can set (it defaults to the endpoint in the WSDL file). So, while this class represents a binding, an instance will represent a port. It has all the required information to get the job done. You may instantiate an object from this class to call the web service, but usually you get an instance from the web service, which is represented by SimpleService_Service:

```
public interface SimpleService_Service extends javax.xml.rpc.Service {
   . . .
   public SimpleService_PortType getSimpleServiceSOAP()
      throws javax.xml.rpc.ServiceException;
   public SimpleService_PortType getSimpleServiceSOAP(java.net.URL portAddress)
      throws javax.xml.rpc.ServiceException;
}
```

Again, it is just an interface. It has a getter for each port defined in that web service. Actually, it has another getter that allows you to specify an endpoint. If we had a port named Foo, then it would have a getFoo() method and a getFoo (URL endpoint) method too. Note that the return type of the getter is the Java interface for the port type (SimpleService_PortType), not the Java class for the binding (SimpleServiceSOAPStub). This is to discourage you from using features specific to the message format or the transport protocol. This way if later the port type is implemented using another binding, your code doesn't need to change.

Having an interface is not enough. You need a concrete class implementing it. SimpleService_ServiceLocator is that:

```
public class SimpleService_ServiceLocator extends org.apache.axis.client.Service
   implements SimpleService_Service {
   public SimpleService_PortType getSimpleServiceSOAP()
```

```
throws javax.xml.rpc.ServiceException {
    ...
}
public SimpleService_PortType getSimpleServiceSOAP(java.net.URL portAddress)
    throws javax.xml.rpc.ServiceException {
    ...
}
}
```

Then create a StubClient.java file in the com.ttdev.simpleservice.client package:

```
public class StubClient {
    public static void main(String[] args)
    throws ServiceException, RemoteException {
    SimpleService_PortType service =
        new SimpleService_ServiceLocator().getSimpleServiceSOAP();
    System.out.println(service.concat(new ConcatRequest("abc", "123")));
    }
}
```

Run it and it should work:

Undeploying a web service

If you'd like to undeploy a web service, you need to send the undeploy.wsdd file (also created by WSDL2Java) to the Axis servlet. This file is simple:

```
<undeployment xmlns="http://xml.apache.org/axis/wsdd/">
  <service name="SimpleServiceSOAP"/>
</undeployment>
```

Note that the root element is <undeployment>, not <deployment>. Listing the service by name is enough. You don't need any other information such as the provider or the operations of the service. To send the content of this file to the Axis servlet, add a target to the build file:

```
<project name="SimpleService">
  ...
  <target name="deploy">
    <axis-admin
      url="http://localhost:8080/Axis/servlet/AxisServlet"
      xmlfile="com/ttdev/simpleservice/deploy.wsdd"/>
  </target>
  <target name="undeploy">
    <axis-admin
      url="http://localhost:8080/Axis/servlet/AxisServlet"
      xmlfile="com/ttdev/simpleservice/undeploy.wsdd"/>
  </target>
</project>
```

Summary

Tomcat hosts one or more web applications. The Axis server is installed as one of the web applications. It in turn hosts one or more web services.

Most usually your input message or output message is sent in a SOAP message. A SOAP message is always an <Envelope> element. It may contain a <Header> which contains one or more header entries/elements. The <Envelope> must contain a <Body> which may contain one or more body entries/elements. For a document style web service, the one and only input message part is usually the single body entry. For a RPC style web service, the element named after the operation will usually contain all message parts and is then included as the single body entry.

To create a web service, you first create a WSDL file describing its interface. This can be done by hand or using a tool like WTP. Then run WSDL2Java on it to generate a service stub. Then fill in the code in the implementation class. Then you need to make the class files available to the Axis server. Then send the content of the deploy.wsdd file to the Axis servlet to tell it to create the web service. The WSDD file specifies the style of the web service, the full name of the implementation class and etc. It also specifies the type of the provider. Axis uses a provider to forward the request to your implementation object.

The endpoint of the deployed web service is http://localhost:8080/<context-path>/services/<name-of-your-service-as-in-the-WSDD-file>.

To undeploy a web service, send the content of the undeploy.wsdd file to the Axis servlet.

To call a web service, run WSDL2Java on the WSDL file to generate a client stub. Then, in your code create a new service locator object which represents a concrete web service. To access the port named "Foo", call getFoo() on it. This will return the port type interface for Foo. Then you can call the methods on it. The client stub will convert the Java data/objects into XML elements, create the request message in the right format and send it to the right endpoint using the right transport protocol.

Chapter 3

Optimizing the development environment

What's in this chapter?

In this chapter you'll learn to optimize the development environment.

Making changes to Java code take effect immediately

At the moment, whenever you make changes to say your web service Java code (SimpleServiceSOAPImpl.java), you will have to copy the class file into the Axis server again. This is troublesome. To solve this problem, you may try to tell Eclipse to put the class files directly into c:\axis\webapps\axis\WEB-INF\classes instead of c:\workspace\SimpleService:

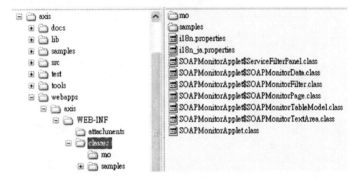

However, as you can see above, Axis also has some of its files in that folder. If you use it as the project output folder, Eclipse may delete those files in some cases (e.g., when you "clean" the project). To be safe than sorry, you can make a clone of the Axis server in your project. To do that, create the following folder structure and copy the indicated files from Axis:

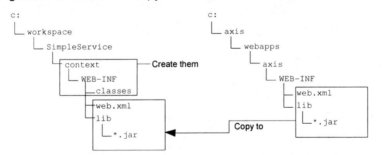

To set the output folder, right click the project in Eclipse and choose "Properties", then choose "Java Build Path" and choose the "Source" tab:

Click "Browse" and choose the "classes" folder you just created:

This way, the class files generated will be put into the context/WEB-INF/classes. While you're in the Build Paths dialog, choose "Excluded: (None)", click Edit and choose the context folder:

This way Eclipse won't try to compile the files in the context folder. Now, you have basically cloned the Axis server into c:\workspace\SimpleService\context. It doesn't have the web pages for human viewing though (so, don't try to access http://localhost:8080/SimpleService and expect to see the Axis front page). It only has the web services related functions.

Finally, you need to register it with Tomcat. To do that, create a file SimpleService.xml in c:\tomcat\conf\Catalina\localhost:

```
<Context
  docBase="c:/workspace/SimpleService/context"
  path="/SimpleService"
  reloadable="true"/>
```

Tell Tomcat to automatically
restart this web application if any
of its class files is changed

As the file name is SimpleService.xml, its context path will be /SimpleService and thus you will access it as http://localhost:8080/SimpleService. Go to the Tomcat Manager to start this web application. As you didn't copy the server-config.wsdd file, you need to modify the deploy target:

```
<project name="SimpleService">
  ...
  <target name="deploy">
    <axis-admin
      url="http://localhost:8080/SimpleService/servlet/AxisServlet"
      xmlfile="com/ttdev/simpleservice/deploy.wsdd"/>
  </target>
</project>
```

Then run it again. To see if it's working, modify StubClient.java:

```
public class StubClient {
  public static void main(String[] args)
      throws ServiceException, RemoteException, MalformedURLException {
    SimpleService_PortType service = new SimpleService_ServiceLocator()
        .getSimpleServiceSOAP(new URL(
            "http://localhost:8080/SimpleService/services/SimpleServiceSOAP"));
    System.out.println(service.concat(new ConcatRequest("abc", "123")));
```

```
      }
   }
```
Run it and it should work. To see if you can change the Java code freely, add
a new parameter to the concat() method:

```
public class SimpleServiceSOAPImpl ... {
   public String concat(ConcatRequest concatRequest) ... {
     return concatRequest.getS1()+" plus "+concatRequest.getS2();
   }
}
```
Then run the client again and it should work:

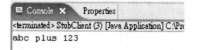

As it's working, change the code back. As the permanent endpoint is changed,
edit the SimpleService.wsdl file to update the endpoint. Don't forget to
generate the client stub again.

Debugging a web service

To debug your web service in Eclipse, you need to set two environment
variables for Tomcat and launch it in a special way (shutdown Tomcat first if
it's running):

Note that you're now launching it using catalina.bat instead of startup.bat. This
way Tomcat will run the JVM in debug mode so that the JVM will listen for
connections on port 8000. Later you'll tell Eclipse to connect to this port. Now,
set a breakpoint here:

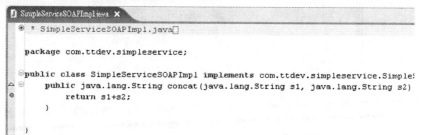

Choose "Debug":

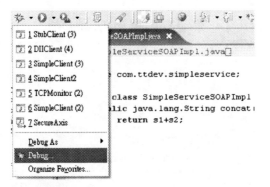

The following window will appear:

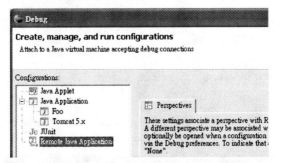

Right click "Remote Java Application" and choose "New". Browse to select your SimpleService project and make sure the port is 8000:

Click "Debug" to connect to the JVM in Tomcat. Now run the StubClient to call the web service. Eclipse will stop at the breakpoint:

Then you can step through the program, check the variables and whatever. To stop the debug session, choose the SimpleService in the Debug window and click the Stop icon:

Having to set all those environment variables every time is not fun. So, you may create a batch file c:\tomcat\bin\debug.bat:

```
set JPDA_ADDRESS=8000
set JPDA_TRANSPORT=dt_socket
catalina jpda start
```

Then in the future you can just run it to start Tomcat.

Summary

To make sure the changes to your Java code take effect immediately, you may make a copy of the Axis server into your own project and set the project output folder to the context/WEB-INF/classes folder. Finally, register it with Tomcat by creating a context descriptor for it. In that context descriptor, set reloadable to true so that it is reloaded whenever class file in its classes folder is changed.

To debug a web service, tell Tomcat to run the JVM in debug mode, set a breakpoint in the Java code and make a Debug configuration in Eclipse to connect to that JVM.

Chapter 4

Understanding the calling process

What's in this chapter?

In this chapter you'll learn what is happening internally when you call a web service.

Calling a web service without a client stub

Suppose that you'd like to call a web service without a client stub. To do that, open the SimpleService project in Eclipse. Create a file DIIClient.java (DII stands for "Dynamic Invocation Interface") in a new com.ttdev.simpleservice.diiclient package:

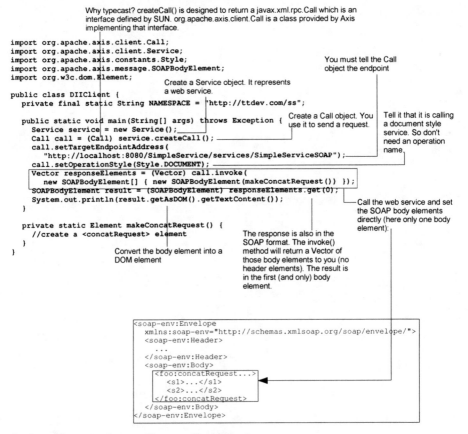

Why typecast? createCall() is designed to return a javax.xml.rpc.Call which is an interface defined by SUN. org.apache.axis.client.Call is a class provided by Axis implementing that interface.

```java
import org.apache.axis.client.Call;
import org.apache.axis.client.Service;
import org.apache.axis.constants.Style;
import org.apache.axis.message.SOAPBodyElement;
import org.w3c.dom.Element;

public class DIIClient {
    private final static String NAMESPACE = "http://ttdev.com/ss";

    public static void main(String[] args) throws Exception {
        Service service = new Service();
        Call call = (Call) service.createCall();
        call.setTargetEndpointAddress(
            "http://localhost:8080/SimpleService/services/SimpleServiceSOAP");
        call.setOperationStyle(Style.DOCUMENT);
        Vector responseElements = (Vector) call.invoke(
            new SOAPBodyElement[] { new SOAPBodyElement(makeConcatRequest()) });
        SOAPBodyElement result = (SOAPBodyElement) responseElements.get(0);
        System.out.println(result.getAsDOM().getTextContent());
    }

    private static Element makeConcatRequest() {
        //create a <concatRequest> element
    }
}
```

Create a Service object. It represents a web service.

You must tell the Call object the endpoint

Create a Call object. You use it to send a request.

Tell it that it is calling a document style service. So don't need an operation name.

Convert the body element into a DOM element

The response is also in the SOAP format. The invoke() method will return a Vector of those body elements to you (no header elements). The result is in the first (and only) body element.

Call the web service and set the SOAP body elements directly (here only one body element):

```xml
<soap-env:Envelope
    xmlns:soap-env="http://schemas.xmlsoap.org/soap/envelope/">
    <soap-env:Header>
        ...
    </soap-env:Header>
    <soap-env:Body>
        <foo:concatRequest...>
            <s1>...</s1>
            <s2>...</s2>
        </foo:concatRequest>
    </soap-env:Body>
</soap-env:Envelope>
```

Define the makeConcatRequest() method:

```
...
import javax.xml.parsers.DocumentBuilder;
import javax.xml.parsers.DocumentBuilderFactory;
import javax.xml.parsers.ParserConfigurationException;
mport org.w3c.dom.Document;
import org.w3c.dom.Element;

public class DIIClient {
  private final static String NAMESPACE = "http://ttdev.com/ss";

  public static void main(String[] args) throws Exception {
    ...                                             Create an XML document builder
  }                                                 factory
  private static Element makeConcatRequest() {
    DocumentBuilderFactory factory = DocumentBuilderFactory.newInstance();
    factory.setNamespaceAware(true);
    DocumentBuilder builder;        └──── Tell it to support namespaces
    try {
      builder = factory.newDocumentBuilder();──── Create a document builder
    } catch (ParserConfigurationException e) {
      throw new RuntimeException(e);
    }                                      ┌──── Create a document
    Document doc = builder.newDocument();
    Element concatRequest = doc.createElementNS(NAMESPACE, "concatRequest");
    Element s1 = doc.createElement("s1");
    s1.setTextContent("abc");
    concatRequest.appendChild(s1);        Create a <concatRequest> element.
    Element s2 = doc.createElement("s2");  Both the namespace and local name
    s2.setTextContent("124");             are specified.
    concatRequest.appendChild(s2);
    return concatRequest;                 Create an <s1> element. As it is
  }                                        unqualified, just specify the local
}                                          name.

              Append <s1> as a child element to
              the <concatRequest>
```

Now run it and it should work.

Seeing the SOAP messages

Next, let's see the actual SOAP messages. Axis comes with a proxy program called "TCP Monitor" to do that. It works like this (see the diagram below). You tell the client to use the TCP Monitor as a proxy. Then when the client needs to send the request message (carried in an HTTP request), it will send it to the proxy (TCP Monitor). Then TCP Monitor will print it to the console and then forward it to the real destination (the web service). When the web service returns a response message, it will return it to the proxy (TCP Monitor). It will print it to the console and then forward it to the client:

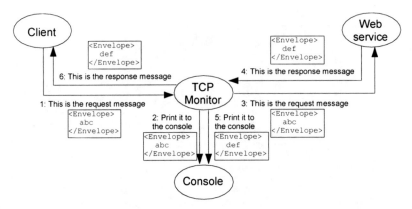

To run TCP Monitor, create a new project with the Axis library (you may copy an existing one) and named it TCPMonitor. Create a TCPMonitor.java:

```
package com.ttdev.tcpmonitor;

import org.apache.axis.utils.tcpmon;

public class TCPMonitor {
  public static void main(String[] args) {
    tcpmon.main(new String[0]);
  }
}
```

Run it and you'll see a new window. Enter any unused port such as 1234 and choose "Proxy":

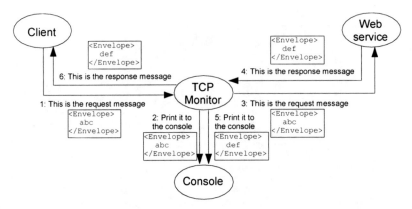

Click "Add". This will open a new tab. Then it will listen on port 1234:

Check the "XML Format" option. This way it will format the content of the HTTP request (the SOAP request but it doesn't know) nicely as XML.

For the client, you need to tell it to use localhost:1234 as the HTTP proxy. To do that, choose the following menu item in Eclipse:

Choose the run configuration for your DIIClient:

Choose the "Arguments" tab and enter the following VM arguments:

Now, run this configuration and you will see the messages in TCP Monitor:

Letting Axis convert the data

At the moment you're passing a SOAP body element to the invoke() method. This works but is quite troublesome. It'd be nice if you can pass it a ConcatRequest object and let the Call object convert it to a <concatRequest>. To do that, first create a ClientConcatRequest.java class (You name it ClientConcatRequest instead of ConcatRequest so that it is clearly your own version, not the version on the server). It should be like:

```java
public class ClientConcatRequest {
  private String s1;
  private String s2;

  public ClientConcatRequest(String s1, String s2) {
    this.s1 = s1;
    this.s2 = s2;
  }
  public String getS1() {
    return s1;
  }
  public String getS2() {
    return s2;
  }
}
```

Then copy DllClient.java and paste it as DllClientAutoConvert.java, then modify it:

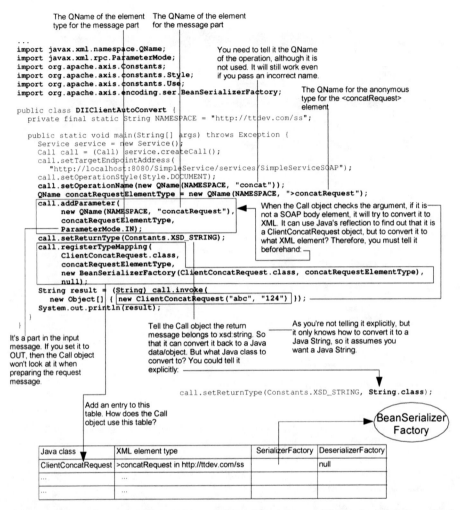

This process of converting a Java value/object to an XML element is called "serialization". On the opposite side, when the client receives an XML element, it will need to convert it to a Java value/object. This process is called "deserialization". In both processes, the table above will be used. The table above in Axis is called the "type mapping registry". Each entry is called a "type mapping".

How does Axis use this type mapping registry? For example (see the diagram below), when you pass a ClientConcatRequest object to the invoke() method, the Call object needs to serialize it into XML. From the addParameter() call it knows that it should be converted to an element named "concatRequest" that belongs to the ">concatRequest" element type. But how to convert it? It will lookup the type mapping registry and find a serializer factory. Then it asks the serializer factory to create a serializer and then asks the latter to perform the serialization. Why not just store a serializer in the registry? It is for performance reason: A serializer factory can cache some common data needed by all the serializers it creates. Anyway, as you have a bean serializer factory in the registry, it will create a bean serializer. It will first output an empty <concatRequest> element as you are telling it the element name. To generate the content of the element, it calls each getter (e.g., getS1()) in the ClientConcatRequest object and use the name of the property ("s1") as the child element name. It will further convert (serialize) the value returned by the getter. As it is a Java String, it looks up the table again (this time it doesn't know the element type) and finds that it can be converted to an xsd:string using a built-in serializer. The result will be the content of the <s1> element. It works similarly for the getS2() getter:

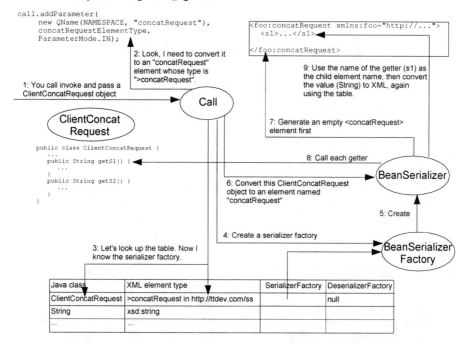

For the bean serializer to work, the ClientConcatRequest class must have a property (getter) named after each child element of <concatRequest>. If you need to receive a <concatRequest>, you should use a bean deserializer. It will create a new ClientConcatRequest object and then for each child element, deserialize it and store the result into the object using a setter. For this to work, your ClientConcatRequest class needs to have a public constructor that takes no argument (called "default constructor") and getters and setters for each field. Such a Java class is called "Java bean". That's why they are called bean serializer and bean deserializer.

Note that you need to register the type mapping in a DII client only. For a client using the generated stub, the stub will do that automatically.

Controlling the ordering of the properties

If you're careful, you may wonder how the bean serializer knows that it should process getS1() before getS2(). It doesn't. It simply processes them in alphabetical order. It means if the <s2> appears before <s1> in the schema, the bean serializer will still generate <s1> first and then <s2> and thus the XML document will become invalid (according to the schema). To solve the problem, modify ClientConcatRequest.java:

```
public class ClientConcatRequest {
    private String s1;
    private String s2;

    public ClientConcatRequest(String s1, String s2) {
        this.s1 = s1;
        this.s2 = s2;
    }
    public String getS1() {
        return s1;
    }
    public String getS2() {
        return s2;
    }
    public static TypeDesc getTypeDesc() {
        TypeDesc td = new TypeDesc(ClientConcatRequest.class);
        ElementDesc s2 = new ElementDesc();
        s2.setFieldName("s2");
        td.addFieldDesc(s2);
        ElementDesc s1 = new ElementDesc();
        s1.setFieldName("s1");
        td.addFieldDesc(s1);
        return td;
    }
}
```

If there is a public static method named getTypeDesc(), then the bean serializer will call it to find out what fields are available and their ordering.

Add a field for "s2" first. You only need to set the field name. Axis will find out the rest.

This is quite a lot of work, right? So, you should use the client stub as long as possible!

Summary

To check the SOAP messages, you can use the TCP Monitor coming with Axis.

To call a web service without using a generated stub, you may use the DII. To use DII, create a Service object and then ask it to create a Call object. Set the various properties of the Call such as the endpoint. Finally, call its invoke() method and provide the parameter values.

If the parameter value is a SOAP body element, it will just send it as is. The return will be just a Vector of SOAP body element. No conversion is required.

Otherwise, it will try to convert the parameter value into XML. This process is called "serialization". For this to work, you need to set the QName of the operation, the name and type of the parameter and the type of the return value. When it receives an XML element, it will try to convert it back into Java data/object. This process is called "deserialization". Given an XML element type or a Java class or both, Axis can determine how to convert between them by looking up the type mapping registry to get a serializer factory or a deserializer factory.

A particular type of mapping is a bean mapping. It uses a bean serializer and a bean deserializer. They assume the Java class is a Java bean and will do their work by serializing or deserializing with its properties. To control the ordering of the properties, you can use a getTypeDesc() method.

You need to register type mappings for Java beans only when using a DII client. A generated stub will do that automatically.

Chapter 5

Accepting multiple parameters

What's in this chapter?

In this chapter you'll learn how to accept multiple parameters in your implementation class.

Accepting multiple parameters

Consider the SimpleServiceSOAPImpl class:

```
public class SimpleServiceSOAPImpl implements SimpleService_PortType{
   public String concat(ConcatRequest concatRequest) ... {
     return concatRequest.getS1()+concatRequest.getS2();
   }
}
```

Because it's a document style web service, you can have a single part in the input message. Therefore, you have a single parameter only. It would be nice if you could:

```
public class SimpleServiceSOAPImpl implements SimpleService_PortType{
   public String concat(String s1, String s2) ... {
     return s1+s2;
   }
}
```

while still accepting a single part (<concatRequest>) in the message. To do that, you just need to make two changes to the WSDL file:

```
<?xml version="1.0" encoding="UTF-8"?>
<wsdl:definitions xmlns:soap="http://schemas.xmlsoap.org/wsdl/soap/"
   xmlns:tns="http://ttdev.com/ss"
   xmlns:wsdl="http://schemas.xmlsoap.org/wsdl/"
   xmlns:xsd="http://www.w3.org/2001/XMLSchema" name="SimpleService"
   targetNamespace="http://ttdev.com/ss">
   <wsdl:types>
     <xsd:schema targetNamespace="http://ttdev.com/ss">
       <xsd:element name="concatRequest concat">
         <xsd:complexType>
           <xsd:sequence>
             <xsd:element name="s1" type="xsd:string"></xsd:element>
             <xsd:element name="s2" type="xsd:string"></xsd:element>
           </xsd:sequence>
         </xsd:complexType>
       </xsd:element>
     </xsd:schema>                          Must update here accordingly
   </wsdl:types>                                       |
   <wsdl:message name="concatRequest">                 |
     <wsdl:part name="concatRequest" element="tns:concatRequest concat" />
   </wsdl:message>
   <wsdl:message name="concatResponse">               Make sure the element name of
     <wsdl:part name="concatResponse" type="xsd:string" />   that single part is the same as
   </wsdl:message>                                      that of the operation.
   <wsdl:portType name="SimpleService">
     <wsdl:operation name="concat">
       <wsdl:input message="tns:concatRequest" />
       <wsdl:output message="tns:concatResponse" />
     </wsdl:operation>
   </wsdl:portType>
   ...
</wsdl:definitions>
```

To test it, copy the SimpleService project and paste it as WrappedService. Delete all the Java files. Rename SimpleService.wsdl to WrappedService.wsdl and modify it:

```
<?xml version="1.0" encoding="UTF-8"?>
```

```
<wsdl:definitions xmlns:soap="http://schemas.xmlsoap.org/wsdl/soap/"
  xmlns:tns="http://ttdev.com/ss"
  xmlns:wsdl="http://schemas.xmlsoap.org/wsdl/"
  xmlns:xsd="http://www.w3.org/2001/XMLSchema" name="WrappedService"
  targetNamespace="http://ttdev.com/ss">
  <wsdl:types>
    <xsd:schema targetNamespace="http://ttdev.com/ss">
      <xsd:element name="concat">
        <xsd:complexType>
          <xsd:sequence>
            <xsd:element name="s1" type="xsd:string"></xsd:element>
            <xsd:element name="s2" type="xsd:string"></xsd:element>
          </xsd:sequence>
        </xsd:complexType>
      </xsd:element>
    </xsd:schema>
  </wsdl:types>
  <wsdl:message name="concatRequest">
    <wsdl:part name="concatRequest" element="tns:concat" />
  </wsdl:message>
  <wsdl:message name="concatResponse">
    <wsdl:part name="concatResponse" type="xsd:string" />
  </wsdl:message>
  <wsdl:portType name="WrappedService">
    <wsdl:operation name="concat">
      <wsdl:input message="tns:concatRequest" />
      <wsdl:output message="tns:concatResponse" />
    </wsdl:operation>
  </wsdl:portType>
  <wsdl:binding name="WrappedServiceSOAP" type="tns:WrappedService">
    <soap:binding style="document"
      transport="http://schemas.xmlsoap.org/soap/http" />
    <wsdl:operation name="concat">
      <soap:operation
        soapAction="http://ttdev.com/ss/NewOperation" />
      <wsdl:input>
        <soap:body parts="concatRequest" use="literal" />
      </wsdl:input>
      <wsdl:output>
        <soap:body parts="concatResponse" use="literal" />
      </wsdl:output>
    </wsdl:operation>
  </wsdl:binding>
  <wsdl:service name="WrappedService">
    <wsdl:port binding="tns:WrappedServiceSOAP"
      name="WrappedServiceSOAP">
      <soap:address
location="http://localhost:8080/WrappedService/services/WrappedServiceSOAP" />
    </wsdl:port>
  </wsdl:service>
</wsdl:definitions>
```

Modify build.xml:

```
<project name="WrappedService">
  <property name="axis.home" value="c:/axis"/>
  <property name="javamail.home" value="c:/javamail-1.3.3_01"/>
  <property name="jaf.home" value="c:/jaf-1.0.2"/>
  <path id="axis.classpath">
    <fileset dir="${axis.home}/lib">
      <include name="**/*.jar" />
    </fileset>
    <fileset dir="${javamail.home}">
      <include name="**/*.jar" />
    </fileset>
    <fileset dir="${jaf.home}">
      <include name="**/*.jar" />
    </fileset>
  </path>
  <taskdef
    resource="axis-tasks.properties"
```

```
  classpathref="axis.classpath" />
<target name="generate-service-stub">
  <axis-wsdl2java
    serverside="true"
    url="WrappedService.wsdl">
    <mapping
      namespace="http://ttdev.com/ss"
      package="com.ttdev.wrappedservice"/>
  </axis-wsdl2java>
</target>
<target name="generate-client-stub">
  <axis-wsdl2java
    url="WrappedService.wsdl">
    <mapping
      namespace="http://ttdev.com/ss"
      package="com.ttdev.wrappedservice.client"/>
  </axis-wsdl2java>
</target>
<target name="deploy">
  <axis-admin
    url="http://localhost:8080/WrappedService/servlet/AxisServlet"
    xmlfile="com/ttdev/wrappedservice/deploy.wsdd"/>
</target>
<target name="undeploy">
  <axis-admin
    url="http://localhost:8080/WrappedService/servlet/AxisServlet"
    xmlfile="com/ttdev/wrappedservice/undeploy.wsdd"/>
</target>
</project>
```

Run build.xml to generate the service stub and client stub. Check the WrappedServiceSOAPImpl.java:

```
public class WrappedServiceSOAPImpl implements WrappedService_PortType {
  public String concat(String s1, String s2) throws java.rmi.RemoteException {
    return null;
  }
}
```

Check deploy.wsdd:

```
<deployment
  xmlns="http://xml.apache.org/axis/wsdd/"
  xmlns:java="http://xml.apache.org/axis/wsdd/providers/java">
  <service name="WrappedServiceSOAP"
    provider="java:RPC" style="wrapped" use="literal">
    <parameter .../>
    <parameter .../>
    ...
  </service>
</deployment>
```

These are the two major changes when WSDL2Java finds that the element of the single part has the same QName as the operation. What does "wrapped" style mean? First of all, this is not really a style in WSDL. The service is still a 100% document style service. The clients can still call it the same way (except that <concatRequest> is changed to <concat>). The difference is how the RPC provider works. When it receives a request message (see the diagram below), it finds that the wrapped convention has been turned on for this service. So, it assumes that the QName of the outermost element should be the same as the operation. So, it uses this element QName to lookup the operation. Then, for each child element, it will deserialize it to get back a Java value/object. So it builds up a list of values. Finally, it calls the concat() method in your back end class and pass that list of values as parameter values:

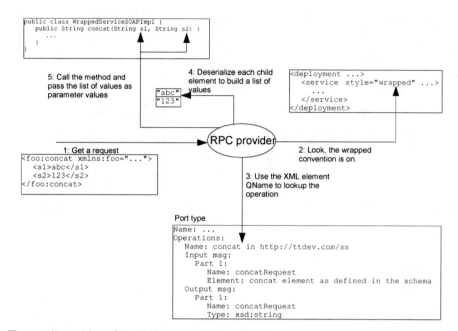

To see it working, fill out the concat() method:

```
public class WrappedServiceSOAPImpl implements WrappedService_PortType {
   public String concat(String s1, String s2) throws java.rmi.RemoteException {
      return s1+s2;
   }
}
```

Delete the server-config.wsdd file. Create a context descriptor WrappedService.xml. Finally, deploy it. Create a StubClient.java in the client package:

```
public class StubClient {
   public static void main(String[] args) throws ServiceException, RemoteException {
      WrappedService_PortType service =
         new WrappedService_ServiceLocator().getWrappedServiceSOAP();
      System.out.println(service.concat("abc", "123"));
   }
}
```

When WSDL2Java generates the client stub, it finds the element and the operation have the same QName, so it changes the method signature accordingly.

```
public interface WrappedService_PortType extends java.rmi.Remote {
   public String concat(String s1, String s2)
      throws java.rmi.RemoteException;
}
```

Run it and it should work. Note that only the method signature has changed. The structure of the request message is not changed at all (except <concatRequest> is changed to <concat>). It means the stub will use the QName of the operation to create an element and then serialize each parameter value as a child element.

Creating a Dll client to call a wrapped service

You could just call it like a document style service (e.g., use a bean serializer).
But you can also call it like this:

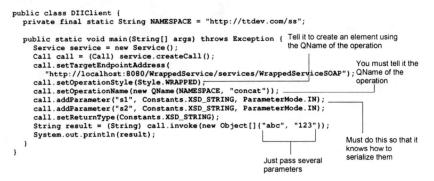

```
public class DIIClient {
    private final static String NAMESPACE = "http://ttdev.com/ss";

    public static void main(String[] args) throws Exception {
        Service service = new Service();
        Call call = (Call) service.createCall();
        call.setTargetEndpointAddress(
            "http://localhost:8080/WrappedService/services/WrappedServiceSOAP");
        call.setOperationStyle(Style.WRAPPED);
        call.setOperationName(new QName(NAMESPACE, "concat"));
        call.addParameter("s1", Constants.XSD_STRING, ParameterMode.IN);
        call.addParameter("s2", Constants.XSD_STRING, ParameterMode.IN);
        call.setReturnType(Constants.XSD_STRING);
        String result = (String) call.invoke(new Object[]{"abc", "123"});
        System.out.println(result);
    }
}
```

Tell it to create an element using the QName of the operation

You must tell it the QName of the operation

Just pass several parameters

Must do this so that it knows how to serialize them

Interoperability

The wrapped convention is a good idea. It is the only kind of web service supported by the .NET framework. Obviously Axis has also implemented this convention. The good news is, from the view point of the caller, it is just a document+literal style service. So if the caller doesn't understand the wrapped convention, it can still access it as a regular document style service.

Summary

You can use the wrapped convention support in WSDL2Java and in the RPC provider so that your back end Java method can have multiple parameters. The clients understanding this convention can also call it using multiple parameters. For those not understanding it, they can still call it as a regular document style service.

To ensure interoperability with .NET, you should use this convention.

Chapter 6

Sending and receiving complex data structures

What's in this chapter?

In this chapter you'll learn how to send and receive complex data structures to and from a web service.

Product query

Suppose that your company would like to use web service to let your customers query the product availability and place orders with you. For this you need to discuss with them to decide on the interface. It doesn't make sense to say that "When doing query, let's send me an object of such a Java class. In this class there are this and that fields..." because perhaps the people involved aren't programmers or don't use Java. Instead, XML is what is designed for this. It is platform neutral and programming language neutral. So, suppose that you all agree on the following schema:

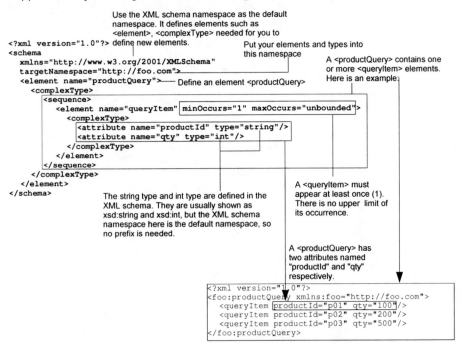

That is, when they need to find out the availability of some products, they will send you a <productQuery> element. For example if they'd like to check if you have 100 pieces of p01, 200 pieces of p02 and 500 pieces of p03, they may send you a request like this:

How does your web service reply? Use an XML element of course. So, in the schema you may have:

```
<?xml version="1.0"?>
<schema
  xmlns="http://www.w3.org/2001/XMLSchema"
  targetNamespace="http://foo.com">
  <element name="productQuery">
    ...
  </element>
  <element name="productQueryResult">      For each <queryItem>, if the product is
    <complexType>                          available, create a <resultItem> telling
      <sequence>                           the unit price.
        <element name="resultItem" minOccurs="1" maxOccurs="unbounded">
          <complexType>
            <attribute name="productId" type="string"/>
            <attribute name="price" type="int"/>
          </complexType>
        </element>
      </sequence>
    </complexType>
  </element>
</schema>
```

So, for the sample query above, if you have over 100 pieces of p01 and 500 pieces of p03 but only 150 pieces of p02, and you're willing to sell p01 at 5 dollars each and p03 at 8 dollars each, you may reply:

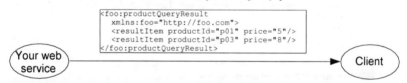

To implement this, create a new project named BizService as usual (You may copy an old one. If so, delete the server-config.wsdd file). Create a context descriptor BizService.xml. Create a BizService.wsdl file (use WTP or by hand):

```
<?xml version="1.0" encoding="UTF-8"?>
<wsdl:definitions xmlns:soap="http://schemas.xmlsoap.org/wsdl/soap/"
  xmlns:tns="http://foo.com"
  xmlns:wsdl="http://schemas.xmlsoap.org/wsdl/"
  xmlns:xsd="http://www.w3.org/2001/XMLSchema" name="BizService"
  targetNamespace="http://foo.com">
  <wsdl:types>
    <xsd:schema targetNamespace="http://foo.com"
      xmlns="http://www.w3.org/2001/XMLSchema">
      <element name="productQuery">
        <complexType>
          <sequence>
            <element name="queryItem" minOccurs="1" maxOccurs="unbounded">
              <complexType>
                <attribute name="productId" type="string" />
                <attribute name="qty" type="int" />
```

```
                    </complexType>
                  </element>
                </sequence>
              </complexType>
            </element>
            <element name="productQueryResult">
              <complexType>
                <sequence>
                  <element name="resultItem" minOccurs="1" maxOccurs="unbounded">
                    <complexType>
                      <attribute name="productId" type="string" />
                      <attribute name="price" type="int" />
                    </complexType>
                  </element>
                </sequence>
              </complexType>
            </element>
          </xsd:schema>
        </wsdl:types>
        <wsdl:message name="queryResponse">
          <wsdl:part name="queryResponse" element="tns:productQueryResult" />
        </wsdl:message>
        <wsdl:message name="queryRequest">
          <wsdl:part element="tns:productQuery" name="queryRequest" />
        </wsdl:message>
        <wsdl:portType name="BizService">
          <wsdl:operation name="query">
            <wsdl:input message="tns:queryRequest" />
            <wsdl:output message="tns:queryResponse" />
          </wsdl:operation>
        </wsdl:portType>
        <wsdl:binding name="BizServiceSOAP" type="tns:BizService">
          <soap:binding style="document"
            transport="http://schemas.xmlsoap.org/soap/http" />
          <wsdl:operation name="query">
            <soap:operation soapAction="http://foo.com/NewOperation" />
            <wsdl:input>
              <soap:body parts="queryRequest" use="literal" />
            </wsdl:input>
            <wsdl:output>
              <soap:body parts="queryResponse" use="literal" />
            </wsdl:output>
          </wsdl:operation>
        </wsdl:binding>
        <wsdl:service name="BizService">
          <wsdl:port binding="tns:BizServiceSOAP" name="BizServiceSOAP">
            <soap:address
              location="http://localhost:8080/BizService/services/BizServiceSOAP" />
          </wsdl:port>
        </wsdl:service>
      </wsdl:definitions>
```

Create a build.xml file:

```
<project name="BizService">
  <property name="axis.home" value="c:/axis"/>
  <property name="javamail.home" value="c:/javamail-1.3.3_01"/>
  <property name="jaf.home" value="c:/jaf-1.0.2"/>
  <path id="axis.classpath">
    <fileset dir="${axis.home}/lib">
      <include name="**/*.jar" />
    </fileset>
    <fileset dir="${javamail.home}">
      <include name="**/*.jar" />
    </fileset>
    <fileset dir="${jaf.home}">
      <include name="**/*.jar" />
    </fileset>
  </path>
```

```
<taskdef
  resource="axis-tasks.properties"
  classpathref="axis.classpath" />
<target name="generate-service-stub">
  <axis-wsdl2java
    serverside="true"
    url="BizService.wsdl">
    <mapping
      namespace="http://foo.com"
      package="com.ttdev.bizservice"/>
  </axis-wsdl2java>
</target>
<target name="generate-client-stub">
  <axis-wsdl2java
    url="BizService.wsdl">
    <mapping
      namespace="http://foo.com"
      package="com.ttdev.bizservice.client"/>
  </axis-wsdl2java>
</target>
<target name="deploy">
  <axis-admin
    url="http://localhost:8080/BizService/servlet/AxisServlet"
    xmlfile="com/ttdev/bizservice/deploy.wsdd"/>
</target>
<target name="undeploy">
  <axis-admin
    url="http://localhost:8080/BizService/servlet/AxisServlet"
    xmlfile="com/ttdev/bizservice/undeploy.wsdd"/>
</target>
</project>
```

Generate the service stub and client stub. Modify the back end service class:

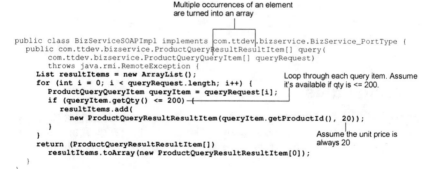

Multiple occurrences of an element are turned into an array

```
public class BizServiceSOAPImpl implements com.ttdev.bizservice.BizService_PortType {
  public com.ttdev.bizservice.ProductQueryResultResultItem[] query(
      com.ttdev.bizservice.ProductQueryQueryItem[] queryRequest)
    throws java.rmi.RemoteException {
    List resultItems = new ArrayList();
    for (int i = 0; i < queryRequest.length; i++) {
      ProductQueryQueryItem queryItem = queryRequest[i];
      if (queryItem.getQty() <= 200)
        resultItems.add(
          new ProductQueryResultResultItem(queryItem.getProductId(), 20));
    }
    return (ProductQueryResultResultItem[])
      resultItems.toArray(new ProductQueryResultResultItem[0]);
  }
}
```

Loop through each query item. Assume it's available if qty is <= 200.

Assume the unit price is always 20

Deploy it. Create a StubClient.java in the client package:

```
public class StubClient {
  public static void main(String[] args)
    throws ServiceException, RemoteException {
    BizService_PortType service =
      new BizService_ServiceLocator().getBizServiceSOAP();
    ProductQueryResultResultItem[] resultItems = service.query(
      new ProductQueryQueryItem[] {
        new ProductQueryQueryItem("p01", 100),
        new ProductQueryQueryItem("p02", 200),
        new ProductQueryQueryItem("p03", 500) });
    for (int i = 0; i < resultItems.length; i++) {
      ProductQueryResultResultItem item = resultItems[i];
      System.out.println(item.getProductId() + ": " + item.getPrice());
    }
  }
}
```

}

Run the client and it should work:

```
Console  ×    Properties
<terminated> StubClient (4) [Java Applic
p01: 20
p02: 20
```

Sending more data in a message

By the way, this query operation demonstrates a good practice in web services: You generally hope to send more data in a message. For example, you may be sending many query items in a single response message. This is more efficient than sending a single query item object in a message. This is because there is a certain overhead involved in sending a message, even if it contains no data:

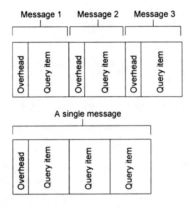

Returning faults

Suppose that a client is calling your query operation but a product id is invalid (not just out of stock, but absolutely unknown) or the quantity is zero or negative. You may want to throw an exception. To do that, modify the WSDL file:

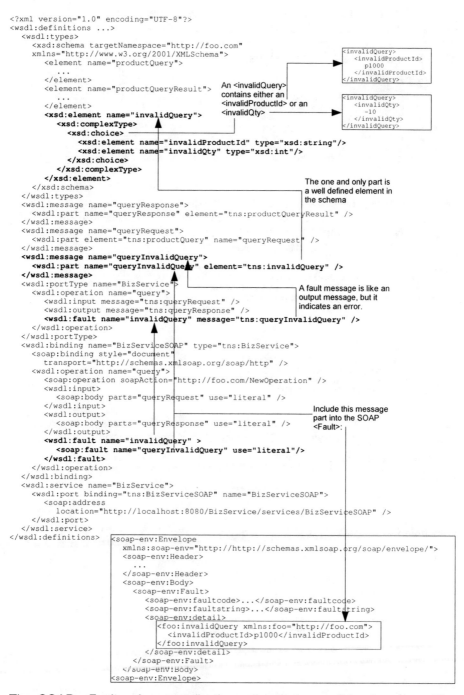

```
<?xml version="1.0" encoding="UTF-8"?>
<wsdl:definitions ...>
  <wsdl:types>
    <xsd:schema targetNamespace="http://foo.com"
    xmlns="http://www.w3.org/2001/XMLSchema">
      <element name="productQuery">
        ...
      </element>
      <element name="productQueryResult">
        ...
      </element>
      <xsd:element name="invalidQuery">
        <xsd:complexType>
          <xsd:choice>
            <xsd:element name="invalidProductId" type="xsd:string"/>
            <xsd:element name="invalidQty" type="xsd:int"/>
          </xsd:choice>
        </xsd:complexType>
      </xsd:element>
    </xsd:schema>
  </wsdl:types>
  <wsdl:message name="queryResponse">
    <wsdl:part name="queryResponse" element="tns:productQueryResult" />
  </wsdl:message>
  <wsdl:message name="queryRequest">
    <wsdl:part element="tns:productQuery" name="queryRequest" />
  </wsdl:message>
  <wsdl:message name="queryInvalidQuery">
    <wsdl:part name="queryInvalidQuery" element="tns:invalidQuery" />
  </wsdl:message>
  <wsdl:portType name="BizService">
    <wsdl:operation name="query">
      <wsdl:input message="tns:queryRequest" />
      <wsdl:output message="tns:queryResponse" />
      <wsdl:fault name="invalidQuery" message="tns:queryInvalidQuery" />
    </wsdl:operation>
  </wsdl:portType>
  <wsdl:binding name="BizServiceSOAP" type="tns:BizService">
    <soap:binding style="document"
    transport="http://schemas.xmlsoap.org/soap/http" />
    <wsdl:operation name="query">
      <soap:operation soapAction="http://foo.com/NewOperation" />
      <wsdl:input>
        <soap:body parts="queryRequest" use="literal" />
      </wsdl:input>
      <wsdl:output>
        <soap:body parts="queryResponse" use="literal" />
      </wsdl:output>
      <wsdl:fault name="invalidQuery" >
        <soap:fault name="queryInvalidQuery" use="literal"/>
      </wsdl:fault>
    </wsdl:operation>
  </wsdl:binding>
  <wsdl:service name="BizService">
    <wsdl:port binding="tns:BizServiceSOAP" name="BizServiceSOAP">
      <soap:address
        location="http://localhost:8080/BizService/services/BizServiceSOAP" />
    </wsdl:port>
  </wsdl:service>
</wsdl:definitions>
```

An <invalidQuery> contains either an <invalidProductId> or an <invalidQty>

```
<invalidQuery>
  <invalidProductId>
    p1000
  </invalidProductId>
</invalidQuery>
```

```
<invalidQuery>
  <invalidQty>
    -10
  </invalidQty>
</invalidQuery>
```

The one and only part is a well defined element in the schema

A fault message is like an output message, but it indicates an error.

Include this message part into the SOAP <Fault>:

```
<soap-env:Envelope
  xmlns:soap-env="http://http://schemas.xmlsoap.org/soap/envelope/">
  <soap-env:Header>
    ...
  </soap-env:Header>
  <soap-env:Body>
    <soap-env:Fault>
      <soap-env:faultcode>...</soap-env:faultcode>
      <soap-env:faultstring>...</soap-env:faultstring>
      <soap-env:detail>
        <foo:invalidQuery xmlns:foo="http://foo.com">
          <invalidProductId>p1000</invalidProductId>
        </foo:invalidQuery>
      </soap-env:detail>
    </soap-env:Fault>
  </soap-env:Body>
<soap-env:Envelope>
```

The SOAP <Fault> element tells the caller that something is wrong. The

<faultcode> is a QName acting as an error code. The <faultstring> is an error message for human reading. The <detail> will contain any information that both sides agree on. In this case, it contains your fault message part. Next, generate the service and client stubs:

```
Console ✕  Properties
<terminated> BizService build.xml [Ant Build] C:\Program Files\Java\jre1.5.0_02\bin\javaw.exe (Dec 31, 2005 9:15:18 PM)
Buildfile: C:\workspace\BizService\build.xml
generate-client-stub:
[axis-wsdl2java]  WSDL2Java C:\workspace\BizService\BizService.wsdl
generate-service-stub:
[axis-wsdl2java]  WSDL2Java C:\workspace\BizService\BizService.wsdl
[axis-wsdl2java] BizServiceSOAPImpl.java already exists, WSDL2Java will not overwrite it.
BUILD SUCCESSFUL
Total time: 1 second
```

Note that it is saying BizServiceSOAPImpl.java already exists, so it won't overwrite it. This is no good. So, you need to copy it to somewhere and then delete it. Now generate the service stub again. Refresh the files and you will see a new Java class InvalidQuery.java:

```
public class InvalidQuery extends org.apache.axis.AxisFault
    implements java.io.Serializable {
    private java.lang.String invalidProductId;
    private java.lang.Integer invalidQty;

    public InvalidQuery() {
    }

    public InvalidQuery(
        java.lang.String invalidProductId,
        java.lang.Integer invalidQty) {
      this.invalidProductId = invalidProductId;
      this.invalidQty = invalidQty;
    } ...
}
```

AxisFault is a class extending RemoteException. So this class is an exception class. The method signature in BizServiceSOAPImpl has also been updated:

```
public class BizServiceSOAPImpl implements BizService_PortType{
   public ProductQueryResultResultItem[] query(
     ProductQueryQueryItem[] queryRequest)
     throws RemoteException, InvalidQuery {
        return null;
     }
}
```

Now put your code back and add some code to validate the query:

```
public class BizServiceSOAPImpl implements BizService_PortType{
   public ProductQueryResultResultItem[] query(
     ProductQueryQueryItem[] queryRequest)
     throws RemoteException, InvalidQuery {
     List resultItems = new ArrayList();
     for (int i = 0; i < queryRequest.length; i++) {
       ProductQueryQueryItem queryItem = queryRequest[i];
       if (!queryItem.getProductId().startsWith("p")) {
         throw new InvalidQuery(queryItem.getProductId(), null);
       }
       if (queryItem.getQty() <= 0) {
         throw new InvalidQuery(null, queryItem.getQty());
       }
       if (queryItem.getQty() <= 200) {
         resultItems.add(
           new ProductQueryResultResultItem(queryItem.getProductId(), 20));
```

```
      }
    }
    return (ProductQueryResultResultItem[])
      resultItems.toArray(new ProductQueryResultResultItem[0]);
}
```

To see if it's working, modify StubClient.java:

```
public class StubClient {
  public static void main(String[] args)
    throws ServiceException, RemoteException {
    try {
      BizService_PortType service = new BizService_ServiceLocator()
        .getBizServiceSOAP();
      ProductQueryResultResultItem[] resultItems = service
        .query(new ProductQueryQueryItem[] {
            new ProductQueryQueryItem("p01", 100),
            new ProductQueryQueryItem("p02", -200),
            new ProductQueryQueryItem("p03", 500) });
      for (int i = 0; i < resultItems.length; i++) {
        ProductQueryResultResultItem item = resultItems[i];
        System.out.println(item.getProductId() + ": " + item.getPrice());
      }
    } catch (InvalidQuery invalidQuery) {
      System.out.println(invalidQuery.getInvalidProductId());
      System.out.println(invalidQuery.getInvalidQty());
    }
  }
}
```

Deploy the service, then run the StubClient and it should work:

If you'd like, you can see the messages in TCP Monitor:

Note that when a client receives a <Fault> element, there is no guarantee that it will deserialize the content of the <detail> element to create an exception object (because the content of the <detail> element is not defined by any standard). So, when returning a fault, keep in mind that although the client should know something is wrong (due to the <Fault>), it may be unable to find out the class of the exception or its fields.

Using encoded

You have been writing document style services. In addition, the parts are sent as "literal":

```xml
<?xml version="1.0" encoding="UTF-8"?>
<wsdl:definitions ...>
  ...
  <wsdl:binding name="BizServiceSOAP" type="tns:BizService">
    <soap:binding style="document"
      transport="http://schemas.xmlsoap.org/soap/http" />
    <wsdl:operation name="query">
      <soap:operation soapAction="http://foo.com/NewOperation" />
      <wsdl:input>
        <soap:body parts="queryRequest" use="literal" />
      </wsdl:input>
      <wsdl:output>
        <soap:body parts="queryResponse" use="literal" />
      </wsdl:output>
      <wsdl:fault name="invalidQuery" >
        <soap:fault name="queryInvalidQuery" use="literal"/>
      </wsdl:fault>
    </wsdl:operation>
  </wsdl:binding>
  ...
</wsdl:definitions>
```

What does literal means? If you don't use literal, you may set it to "encoded". Then Axis will perform some extra encoding of the data in order to convert it into XML. For example, it will be able to handle multi-dimension arrays and data structures containing loops (e.g., a circular linked-list). These kind of data structures don't have direct counter-parts in XML. In fact, if you start from a WSDL, you will never get these data types from WSDL2Java. So, "encoded" is useful only when you have some legacy code that uses such data structures and you'd like to expose it as a web service.

The resulting XML is XML but can't be validated by any schema. This is prohibited in document style services. Therefore, in order to use "encoded", you must use the RPC style.

To use RPC+encoded, after changing the WSDL, just generate the stubs again, deploy it again and it will work. You won't notice any difference unless you look at the messages or encounter interoperability problems (remember, RPC style is not good for interoperability).

Summary

You can freely use XML schema elements to express complex data structures. WSDL2Java will translate them into Java types.

For better performance, you should design the interfaces of your web service operations so that more data is sent in a message.

To throw an exception, add a fault message to the port type and add a corresponding child element in the binding. There is no guarantee that the client will be able to get back the exception object unless it is also using Axis.

If you need to send weird data structures, you can use RPC+encoded but interoperability will be affected.

Chapter 7

Sending binary files

What's in this chapter?

In this chapter you'll learn how to receive and return binary files in your web service.

Providing the image of a product

Suppose that you'd like to have a web service to allow people to upload the image (jpeg) of a product (identified by a product id). The problem is that a SOAP message is an XML element and XML is not good at including binary data. You could encode the data say using base64 or something like that, but the encoded data will be much larger than the binary version. This wastes processing time, network bandwidth and transmission time. In fact, if the image is huge, then many XML parsers may not be able to handle it properly. To solve the problem, the idea is that the binary file can be sent outside the SOAP message but in the same HTTP request:

HTTP request

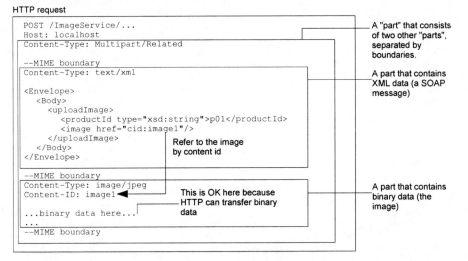

This protocol is called "SOAP with Attachments (SwA)". This is not the greatest way to send attachments. For example, for the <image href="..."> element above, there is no schema element defined for it. This means that you can't use SwA with a document style web service (so use RPC style). There are better standards out there. However, many products don't support them yet.

To implement this image upload operation, create a new project named ImageService as usual (You may copy an old one. If so, delete the server-config.wsdd file). Create a context descriptor ImageService.xml. Modify the WSDL file:

```xml
<?xml version="1.0" encoding="UTF-8"?>
<wsdl:definitions xmlns:soap="http://schemas.xmlsoap.org/wsdl/soap/"
  xmlns:mime="http://schemas.xmlsoap.org/wsdl/mime/"
  xmlns:tns="urn:ttdev.com:imageservice"
  xmlns:wsdl="http://schemas.xmlsoap.org/wsdl/"
  xmlns:xsd="http://www.w3.org/2001/XMLSchema" name="ImageService"
  targetNamespace="urn:ttdev.com:imageservice">
  <wsdl:types>
    <xsd:schema targetNamespace="urn:ttdev.com:imageservice"
      xmlns:tns="urn:ttdev.com:imageservice">
    </xsd:schema>
  </wsdl:types>
  <wsdl:message name="uploadImageResponse" />
  <wsdl:message name="uploadImageRequest">
    <wsdl:part name="productId" type="xsd:string" />
    <wsdl:part name="image" type="xsd:base64Binary" />
  </wsdl:message>
  <wsdl:portType name="ImageService">
    <wsdl:operation name="uploadImage">
      <wsdl:input message="tns:uploadImageRequest" />
      <wsdl:output message="tns:uploadImageResponse" />
    </wsdl:operation>
  </wsdl:portType>
  <wsdl:binding name="ImageServiceSOAP" type="tns:ImageService">
    <soap:binding style="rpc"
      transport="http://schemas.xmlsoap.org/soap/http" />
    <wsdl:operation name="uploadImage">
      <soap:operation soapAction="http://ttdev.com" />
      <wsdl:input>
        <mime:multipartRelated>
          <mime:part>
            <soap:body parts="productId" use="literal" />
          </mime:part>
          <mime:part>
            <mime:content part="image" type="image/jpeg" />
          </mime:part>
        </mime:multipartRelated>
      </wsdl:input>
      <wsdl:output>
        <soap:body parts="" use="literal" />
      </wsdl:output>
    </wsdl:operation>
  </wsdl:binding>
  <wsdl:service name="ImageService">
    <wsdl:port binding="tns:ImageServiceSOAP"
      name="ImageServiceSOAP">
      <soap:address
        location="http://localhost:8080/ImageService/services/ImageServiceSOAP" />
    </wsdl:port>
  </wsdl:service>
</wsdl:definitions>
```

Annotations: The mime prefix is defined here. The operation doesn't return anything, so there is zero part in the output message. It seems to state that this is an element whose content is some base64 encoded binary data. But actually it will be empty and will have a href attribute referring to the attachment part instead. RPC style. There are two parts inside this MIME multipart. This is the first part. Put the SOAP message into this MIME part and put the "productId" message part into the SOAP body. Usually you have a <soap:body> here telling people to put the message part into the <Body> of a SOAP message. But here, you're telling people to put the parts into a MIME Multipart/Related. Put the "image" message part into this MIME part. Set the content to image/jpeg.

Update build.xml:

```xml
<project name="ImageService">
  ...
  <target name="generate-service-stub">
    <axis-wsdl2java
      serverside="true"
      url="ImageService.wsdl">
      <mapping
        namespace="urn:ttdev.com:imageservice"
        package="com.ttdev.imageservice"/>
    </axis-wsdl2java>
  </target>
  <target name="generate-client-stub">
    <axis-wsdl2java
      url="ImageService.wsdl">
      <mapping
        namespace="urn:ttdev.com:imageservice"
        package="com.ttdev.imageservice.client"/>
    </axis-wsdl2java>
  </target>
  <target name="deploy">
    <axis-admin
```

```
      url="http://localhost:8080/ImageService/servlet/AxisServlet"
      xmlfile="com/ttdev/imageservice/deploy.wsdd"/>
  </target>
  <target name="undeploy">
    <axis-admin
      url="http://localhost:8080/ImageService/servlet/AxisServlet"
      xmlfile="com/ttdev/imageservice/undeploy.wsdd"/>
  </target>
</project>
```

Generate the service stub and client stub. Check the implementation class:

```
public interface ImageService_PortType extends java.rmi.Remote {
  public void uploadImage(java.lang.String productId, java.awt.Image image)
    throws java.rmi.RemoteException;
}
```

The image/jpeg MIME part will be converted into a java.awt.Image object for you to use. In the implementation class you may display it or save it or whatever. If you set the content type to say application/octet-stream, then it will become an OctetStream object which can be used like this:

```
import org.apache.axis.attachments.OctetStream;

public class ImageServiceSOAPImpl
  implements com.ttdev.imageservice.ImageService_PortType{
  public void uploadImage(String productId, OctetStream image)
    throws RemoteException {
    byte[] bytes = image.getBytes();
  }
}
```

If you set the MIME type to something that Axis doesn't know such as image/tiff or application/pdf (do it now) and generate the stubs again, then it will always use the DataHandler class:

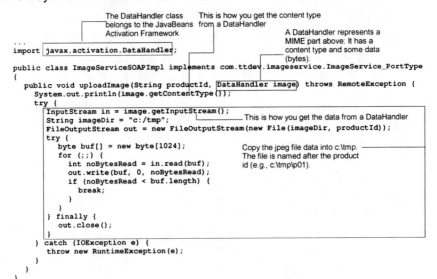

Create a StubClient.java file in the client package:

```
public class StubClient {
    public static void main(String[] args)
        throws ServiceException, RemoteException, MalformedURIException, MalformedURLException {
        ImageService_PortType service = new ImageService_ServiceLocator().getImageServiceSOAP();
        DataSource source = new FileDataSource("c:/axis/docs/images/axis.jpg");
        DataHandler handler = new DataHandler(source);
        service.uploadImage("p01", handler);
        System.out.println("Done!");
    }
}
```

Make sure this file exists

Create a DataHandler object that reads that DataSource object

Create a DataSource object that will read the data from the file. It will also find out the MIME type (image/jpeg in this case) from the file extension (.jpg).

Deploy the service. Create the c:\tmp folder. Run the client. Then check c:\tmp and you should find a new file p01 is there. You can verify that it's a copy of axis.jpg by opening it in a browser:

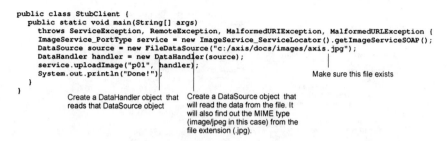

Interoperability

If you need to send binary files with .NET clients or servers, you'll face a problem: .NET doesn't use the MIME format you saw above. Instead, it uses a slightly different format called "DIME". The Axis server is very open-minded: If it receives an attachment in the DIME format, it can still process it and your back end service object won't even notice it at all. But if you're the client and would like to send to a .NET server, by default it won't work:

To solve the problem, you'll have to tell the stub to use the DIME format:

```
                                    Typecast it to the stub. Only the stub
                                    has the _setProperty() method. The
                                    port type only has the business
                                    methods.
public class StubClient {
   public static void main(String[] args) throws ServiceException,
       RemoteException, MalformedURIException, MalformedURLException {
      ImageServiceSOAPStub service = (ImageServiceSOAPStub)
         new ImageService_ServiceLocator().getImageServiceSOAP();
      service._setProperty(                              Tell Axis to use DIME
         Call.ATTACHMENT_ENCAPSULATION_FORMAT,
         Call.ATTACHMENT_ENCAPSULATION_FORMAT_DIME);
      DataSource source = new FileDataSource("c:/axis/docs/images/axis.jpg");
      DataHandler handler = new DataHandler(source);
      service.uploadImage("p01", handler);
      System.out.println("Done!");
   }
}
```

Summary

To receive or send a binary file as an attachment, use a message part that is of type xsd:base64Binary. In the binding, specify that it uses a MIME Multipart/Related part which contains the SOAP message in one MIME part and the binary file in another MIME part. You need to use RPC style web service.

In your implementation class, the attachment will appear as an Image (if the content type is image/jpeg), an OctetStream (for application/octet-stream) or a DataHandler (for others).

To send a binary file to a .NET server, you need to use the DIME format.

Chapter 8

Controlling the life cycle of your back end service object

What's in this chapter?

In this chapter you'll learn how to control the life cycle of your back end service object.

A counter web service

Suppose that you'd like to create a web service that will return a counter. At the beginning it is set to 0. Whenever a client calls it, it will increase the counter and return the new value to the client. To do that, create a new project named CounterService as usual (You may copy an old one. If so, delete the server-config.wsdd file). Update the build.xml file. Create a context descriptor CounterService.xml. Modify CounterService.wsdl:

```xml
<?xml version="1.0" encoding="UTF-8"?>
<wsdl:definitions xmlns:soap="http://schemas.xmlsoap.org/wsdl/soap/"
  xmlns:tns="http://ttdev.com/ss"
  xmlns:wsdl="http://schemas.xmlsoap.org/wsdl/"
  xmlns:xsd="http://www.w3.org/2001/XMLSchema" name="CounterService"
  targetNamespace="http://ttdev.com/ss">
  <wsdl:types>
    <xsd:schema targetNamespace="http://ttdev.com/ss"/>
  </wsdl:types>
  <wsdl:message name="getResponse">
    <wsdl:part name="getResponse" type="xsd:int" />
  </wsdl:message>
  <wsdl:message name="getRequest"/>
  <wsdl:portType name="CounterService">
    <wsdl:operation name="get">
      <wsdl:input message="tns:getRequest" />
      <wsdl:output message="tns:getResponse" />
    </wsdl:operation>
  </wsdl:portType>
  <wsdl:binding name="CounterServiceSOAP" type="tns:CounterService">
    <soap:binding style="document"
      transport="http://schemas.xmlsoap.org/soap/http" />
    <wsdl:operation name="get">
      <soap:operation
        soapAction="http://ttdev.com/get" />
      <wsdl:input>
        <soap:body use="literal" />
      </wsdl:input>
      <wsdl:output>
        <soap:body parts="getResponse" use="literal" />
      </wsdl:output>
    </wsdl:operation>
  </wsdl:binding>
  <wsdl:service name="CounterService">
    <wsdl:port binding="tns:CounterServiceSOAP"
      name="CounterServiceSOAP">
      <soap:address
 location="http://localhost:8080/CounterService/services/CounterServiceSOAP" />
    </wsdl:port>
  </wsdl:service>
</wsdl:definitions>
```

Nothing special here. Generate the service stub and client stub. Modify the implementation class:

```
public class CounterServiceSOAPImpl implements
  com.ttdev.counterservice.CounterService_PortType {
```

```
private int counter = 0;

public int get() throws java.rmi.RemoteException {
    counter++;
    return counter;
}
}
```

Then create a StubClient in the client package:

```
public class StubClient {
    public static void main(String[] args) throws ServiceException,
        RemoteException {
    CounterService_PortType service =
        new CounterService_ServiceLocator().getCounterServiceSOAP();
    System.out.println(service.get());
    System.out.println(service.get());
    System.out.println(service.get());
    }
}
```

Deploy the service and then run the client. Then you'll see:

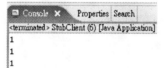

Why it is not 1, 2, 3? Try again:

No matter how many times you run it, it is still 1, 1, 1. Why? This is because by default the java:RPC provider will create a new instance of your back end service class for each request. Isn't this too silly? No. This way if there are two requests arriving at the same time, two back end service objects will be used to serve each and therefore your service objects don't need to be concerned with concurrency issues (unless they try to access some shared resources such as a static variable or a database).

Using an application scoped service object

To solve the problem at hand, you may tell the provider to create a single back end service object and use it for all requests. To do that, modify the deploy.wsdd file:

```
<deployment ...>
  <service name="CounterServiceSOAP" provider="java:RPC" style="document" use="literal">
    <parameter name="className" value="com.ttdev.counterservice.CounterServiceSOAPImpl"/>
    ...
    <parameter name="scope" value="Application"/>
  </service>
</deployment>
```

A back end service object for the whole application.
By default, it is "Request".

Deploy it again. Now, run the client and you'll see:

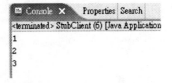

Run it again, you'll see:

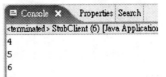

However, there is a bug in the code. As you're using a single object to serve all requests, it must be prepared to handle concurrency issues. For example, it should be modified like:

```
public class CounterServiceSOAPImpl
  implements com.ttdev.counterservice.CounterService_PortType {
  private int counter = 0;

  public synchronized int get() throws java.rmi.RemoteException {
    counter++;
    return counter;
  }
}
```

Of course normally you should not just synchronize the whole method. Instead, you should try to synchronize as little code as possible to allow the requests to run concurrently.

Using a session scoped service object

What if you'd like to allow each client program to have its own counter as shown in the diagram below?

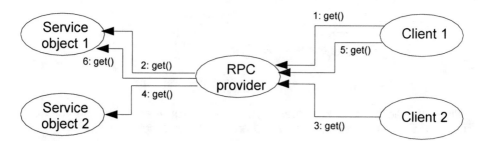

To achieve this effect, you can use the "Session" scope:

```
<deployment ...>
  <service name="CounterServiceSOAP" ...>
    ...
    <parameter name="scope" value="Session"/>
  </service>
</deployment>
```

Deploy it again. However, by default the client has the session support disabled. To enable it:

```
public class StubClient {
   public static void main(String[] args) throws ServiceException,
       RemoteException {
      CounterServiceSOAPStub service = (CounterServiceSOAPStub)
         new CounterService_ServiceLocator().getCounterServiceSOAP();
      service.setMaintainSession(true);
      System.out.println(service.get());
      System.out.println(service.get());
      System.out.println(service.get());
   }
}
```

Now, run it and it should work:

If you run it again, it will appear as a new client, so you'll see:

How does it work? For example, when the client first contacts the Axis server, the server assigns a random id (e.g., 1234) to it. As the maintain session flag has been set to true, the client will remember this as its id. On the subsequent contacts, it will send the id along with the requests. This way the Axis server will be able to identify it as a returning client:

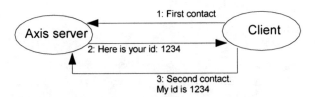

When the client terminates, the id is lost. If you run it again, the server won't recognize it and will assign it a new id and treat it as a new client.

However, this concept of session is supported by Axis only. It is not in web services standards and thus there is no guarantee that it will work with other clients.

Summary

By default, a new back end service object is created to serve each request, so that you don't need to worry about concurrency issues. If you'd like to have a single service object to serve all requests, set the scope to application in the WSDD file. In that case you need to make sure it is thread-safe. If you'd like, you can also set the scope to session so that each client will get its own service object. However, this feature is Axis specific.

Chapter 9

Signing and encrypting SOAP messages

What's in this chapter?

In this chapter you'll learn how to sign and encrypt SOAP messages.

Private key and public key

Usually when you encrypt some text using a key, you need the same key to decrypt it:

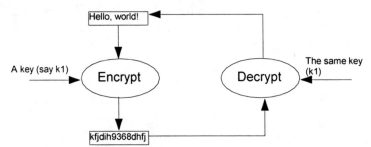

This is called "symmetric encryption". If you would like to send something to me in private, then we need to agree on a key. If you need to send something private to 100 individuals, then you'll need to negotiate with each such individual to agree on a key (so 100 keys in total). This is troublesome.

To solve the problem, an individual may use something called a "private key" and a "public key". First, he uses some software to generate a pair of keys: One is the private key and the other is the public key. There is an interesting relationship between these two keys: If you use the private key to encrypt something, then it can only be decrypted using the public key (using the private key won't work). The reverse is also true: If you use the public key to encrypt something, then it can only be decrypted using the private key:

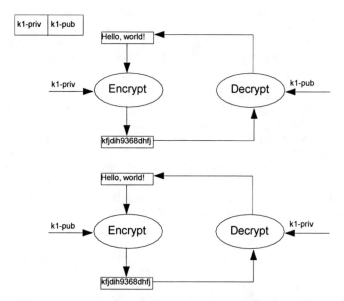

After generating the key pair, he will keep the private key really private (won't tell anyone), but he will tell everyone his public key. Can other people find out the private key from the public key? It is extremely difficult, so there is no worry about it. Now, suppose that you'd like to send something confidential to an individual Paul (see the diagram below), you can use his public key to encrypt it. Even though other people know his public key, they can't decrypt it (as it is encrypted using the public key, only the private key can decrypt it). Only Paul knows the private key and so only he can decrypt it:

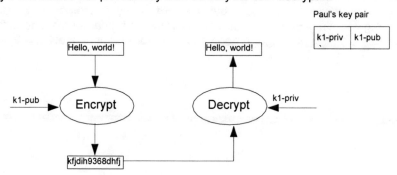

This kind of encryption is called "asymmetric encryption".

Digital signature

Suppose that the message you send to Paul is not confidential. However, Paul really needs to be sure that it is really from you. How to do that? You need to prove to Paul that the creator of the message knows your private key. If he does, then he must be you (remember, nobody else is supposed to know your private key). To prove that, you can use your private key to encrypt the message, then send it to Paul. Paul can try to decrypt it using your public key. If it works, then the creator of the message must know your private key and must be you.

However, this is not a good solution, because if the message is long, the encrypted message may double in size and the encryption takes a lot of time. To solve this problem, you can feed the message to a "one way hash function" (see the diagram below). No matter how long the input is, the output from the one way hash function is always the same small size (e.g., 128 bits). In addition, if two input messages are different (maybe just a single bit is different), then the output will be completely different. Therefore, the output message can be considered a small-sized snapshot of the input message. It is therefore called the "message digest" of the original message:

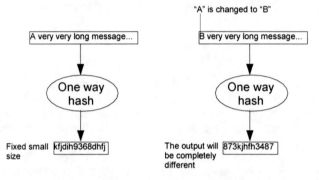

Another feature of the one way hash function is that it is very fast to calculate the digest of a given message, but it is extremely difficult to calculate a message given a digest. Otherwise people would find different messages for a given digest and it is no longer a good snapshot for the message:

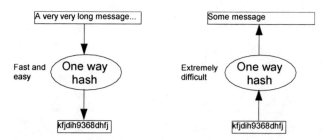

Now, to prove to Paul that you know your private key, you can use your private encrypt to encrypt the message digest (because the digest is small, the result is also small and the encryption process will be fast), then send both the message and the message digest to Paul. He can try to decrypt the digest using your public key. Then he can calculate the digest from the message and compare the two. If the two match, then the person producing the encrypted digest must be you:

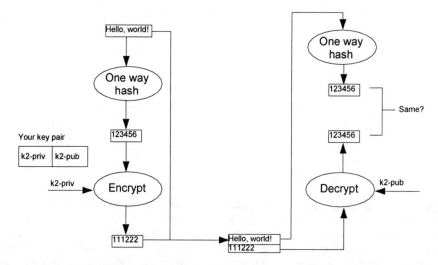

The encrypted digest is called the "digital signature". The whole process of calculating the digest and then encrypting it is called "signing the message".

Signing and encrypting

What if you'd like to sign the message, while keeping the message available to Paul only? Just sign it as usual (see the diagram below) and then encrypt the message and the digest using Paul's public key. When Paul receives it, he uses his private key to decrypt it and then go on to verify the signature as usual:

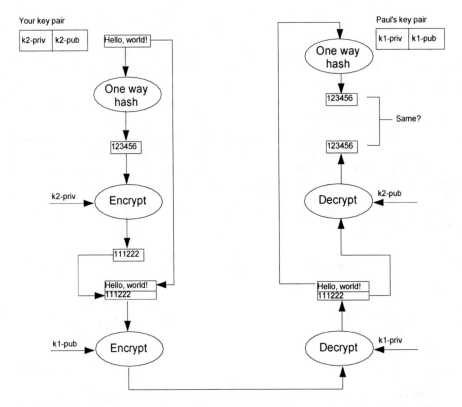

Certificate and CA

This seems to work very well. However, when you need to say send a confidential message to Paul, you'll need his public key. But how can you find out his public key? You can call him on the phone to ask him. But how can you be sure that the person on the phone is really Paul? If he is a hacker, he will tell you his public key. When you send the message to Paul using the hacker's public key, the hacker will be able to decrypt it using his private key.

If you need to communicate with many different individuals, this will get even more troublesome. To solve the problem, Paul may go to a government authority, show them his ID card and etc and tell the authority his public key. Then the authority will generate an electronic message (like an email) stating Paul's public key. Finally, it signs that message using its own private key:

```
Name: Paul
Public key: 666888
                    Signature
```

Such a signed message is called a "certificate". That authority is called a "certificate authority (CA)". Then Paul can put his certificate on his personal web site, email it to you directly or put it onto some 3rd party public web site. From where you get the certificate is unimportant. What is important is that if you can verify the signature of that CA and you trust what the CA says, then you can trust that public key in the certificate. In order to verify the signature, you will need to public key of that CA. What?! You're back to the origin of the problem. However, you only need to find out a single public key for a single entity (the CA), not a public key for everyone you need to communicate with. How to obtain that public key? Usually it is already configured in your browser or you can download it from a trusted web site, newspaper or other sources that you trust.

A CA doesn't really need to be a government authority. It can be well known commercial organizations such as VeriSign.

It means that in order to use asymmetric encryption and digital signature, people need private keys, public keys, a CA and certificates. All these elements combined together is called a "public key infrastructure (PKI)" because it provides a platform for us to use public keys.

Distinguished name

If you review the certificate:

Name: Paul
Public key: 666888
                              Signature

You will see that it is not that useful because there are probably millions of people named "Paul" in the world. Therefore, in a real certificate, usually the country, city and the company of that individual are also included like:

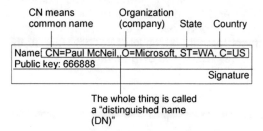

Now if you're looking for the public key of Paul McNeil who works at IBM, you know that the certificate above should NOT be used.

Performance issue with asymmetric encryption

Suppose that you'd like to send an encrypted message to Paul. You can use Paul's public key to do that. However, in practice few people would do it this way, because asymmetric encryption is very slow. In contrast, symmetric encryption is a lot faster. To solve this problem, you can generate a random symmetric key, use it to encrypt the message, then use Paul's public key to encrypt that symmetric key and send it to Paul along with the encrypted message. Paul can use his private key to get back the symmetric key and then use it to decrypt the message:

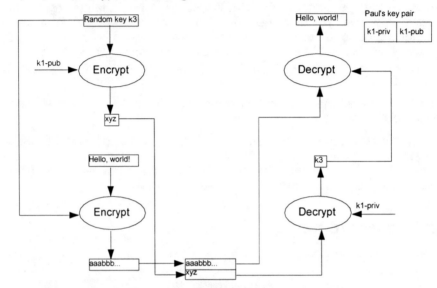

Keeping key pair and certificates in Java

In order to use PKI, typically you should have a private key for yourself (see the diagram below), a certificate for yourself so that you can send to others, a certificate for each person that you need to send something confidential to (e.g., Paul and Mary) and the public keys of the CA's that you trust. For the public key of the CA, you don't directly store its public key. Instead, you store its certificate which contains its public key. But who issued that certificate to it? It was issued by itself (signed by its own private key):

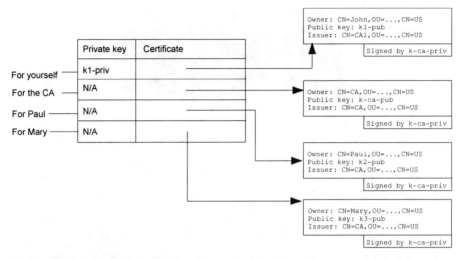

Such a table is called a "keystore" in Java (see the diagram below). A keystore is stored in a file. In addition, each entry in the table has a name called the "alias" of the entry. This way you can, e.g., tell the software to sign a particular message using the private key in the "john" entry (yourself), or encrypt the message using the public key in "paul" entry. Without the alias you will have to use the DN to reference to an entry.

keystore

Alias	Private key	Certificate
john	k1-priv	──────▶
CA	N/A	──────▶
paul	N/A	──────▶
mary	N/A	──────▶

Generating a key pair

In order to generate a key pair, you can use the keytool program in JDK. For example, if your JDK is in c:\Program Files\Java\jdk, then you can find keytool.exe in the bin sub-folder (i.e., c:\Program Files\Java\jdk\bin). For convenience, let's add c:\Program Files\Java\jdk\bin to the PATH:

Note that this PATH setting affects this command prompt only. If later you use a new command prompt, you'll need to set the PATH again. Next, create a folder c:\keys to hold the keys and change into there:

Now, generate a key pair:

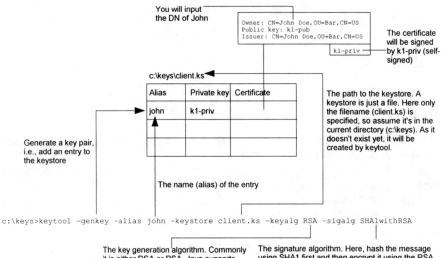

You will input the DN of John

```
Owner: CN=John Doe,OU=Bar,CN=US
Public key: k1-pub
Issuer: CN=John Doe,OU=Bar,CN=US
```

The certificate will be signed by k1-priv (self-signed)

k1-priv

c:\keys\client.ks

Alias	Private key	Certificate
john	k1-priv	

The path to the keystore. A keystore is just a file. Here only the filename (client.ks) is specified, so assume it's in the current directory (c:\keys). As it doesn't exist yet, it will be created by keytool.

Generate a key pair, i.e., add an entry to the keystore

The name (alias) of the entry

```
c:\keys>keytool -genkey -alias john -keystore client.ks -keyalg RSA -sigalg SHA1withRSA
```

The key generation algorithm. Commonly it is either DSA or RSA. Java supports both but some of the libraries you use later only support RSA, so use it here.

The signature algorithm. Here, hash the message using SHA1 first and then encrypt it using the RSA private key. If you don't specify it here, keytool will use MD5withRSA. But MD5 is known to be insecure nowadays, so don't use MD5 anymore.

Let's run it:

You need to provide a keystore password to protect the keystore. You can consider that keytool will append this password to the content of the keystore and then generate a hash and store it into the keystore. If someone modifies the keystore without this password, he won't be able to update the hash. The next time you run keytool on this keystore, it will note the mismatch and warn you not to use this keystore anymore.

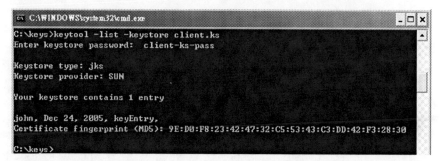

```
C:\WINDOWS\system32\cmd.exe                                          _ □ ×

C:\keys>keytool -genkey -alias john -keystore client.ks -keyalg RSA -sigalg SHA1
withRSA
Enter keystore password:  client-ks-pass
What is your first and last name?
  [Unknown]:  John Doe
What is the name of your organizational unit?
  [Unknown]:                              The DN of John
What is the name of your organization?
  [Unknown]:  Bar
What is the name of your City or Locality?
  [Unknown]:
What is the name of your State or Province?
  [Unknown]:
What is the two-letter country code for this unit?
  [Unknown]:  US
Is CN=John Doe, OU=Unknown, O=Bar, L=Unknown, ST=Unknown, C=US correct?
  [no]:  yes

Enter key password for <john>
       (RETURN if same as keystore password):  john-pass

C:\keys>
```

You need to provide an entry password to protect the entry for John. You can consider that keytool will use this password to encrypt John's private key. This way other people won't be able to read John's private key.

To verify that the entry has been added, you can list the entries:

```
C:\WINDOWS\system32\cmd.exe                                          _ □ ×

C:\keys>keytool -list -keystore client.ks
Enter keystore password:  client-ks-pass

Keystore type: jks
Keystore provider: SUN

Your keystore contains 1 entry

john, Dec 24, 2005, keyEntry,
Certificate fingerprint (MD5): 9E:D0:F8:23:42:47:32:C5:53:43:C3:DD:42:F3:28:30

C:\keys>
```

Note that it asks for the keystore password so that it can verify the hash. If you'd like to see more details in the entries, use the -v option:

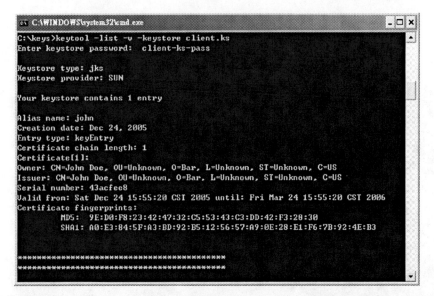

You can see that both the "Owner" and the "Issuer" are set to the DN of John. It shows that it is indeed a self-signed certificate. Having a self-signed certificate is not useful. You need to ask a CA to sign it. To do that, generate a certificate request first:

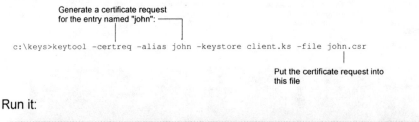

Generate a certificate request
for the entry named "john": ─

```
c:\keys>keytool -certreq -alias john -keystore client.ks -file john.csr
```

Put the certificate request into
this file

Run it:

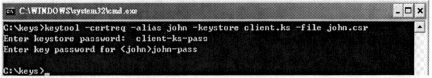

```
C:\keys>keytool -certreq -alias john -keystore client.ks -file john.csr
Enter keystore password:  client-ks-pass
Enter key password for <john>john-pass

C:\keys>
```

Now it has put the certificate request into c:\keys\john.csr. You need to send to a CA. In real life, you should send it to VeriSign or some well known CA to get a certificate (of course a payment is required). Here you'll setup your own CA.

Setting up a CA

Go to http://www.openssl.org/related/binaries.html to download the Windows version of OpenSSL. Suppose the file is Win32OpenSSL-v0.9.8a.exe. Login as the Administrator and run it. Follow the instruction to complete the installation. Suppose that it has been installed into c:\OpenSSL. To make it easier to run, add c:\OpenSSL\bin to the PATH:

Next, create a folder say c:\CA to contain the files of the CA. Then create a private key for the CA itself:

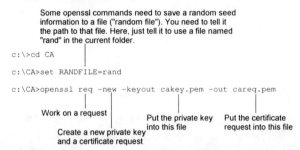

Run it and it will prompt you for the DN of the CA and a password to encrypt the private key (e.g., you may use "ca-pass"):

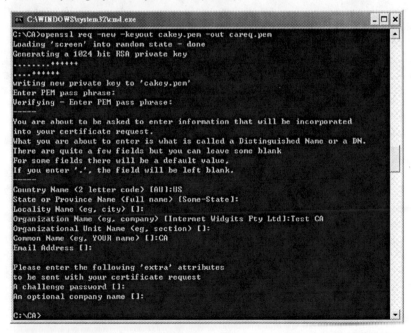

Next, generate a self signed certificate for it:

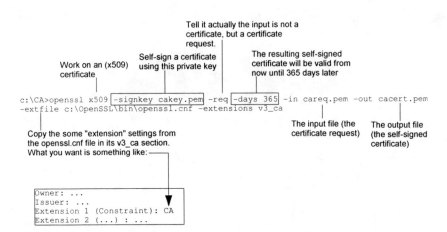

Run it and enter "ca-pass" as the password for the CA key:

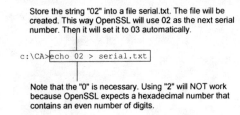

Now you're about to use this CA to sign the certificate request from John (john.csr). However, before that, you need to note that when a CA issues a new certificate, it will put a unique serial number into that certificate. So you need to tell OpenSSL what is the next serial number to use. To do that:

Store the string "02" into a file serial.txt. The file will be created. This way OpenSSL will use 02 as the next serial number. Then it will set it to 03 automatically.

```
c:\CA>echo 02 > serial.txt
```

Note that the "0" is necessary. Using "2" will NOT work because OpenSSL expects a hexadecimal number that contains an even number of digits.

To sign John's certificate request:

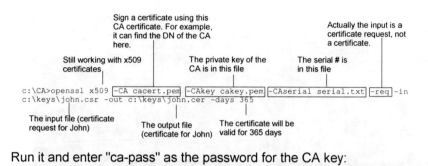

Run it and enter "ca-pass" as the password for the CA key:

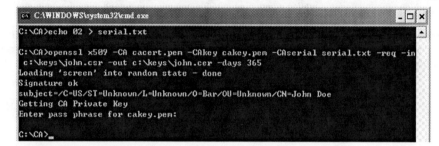

Importing the certificate into the keystore

Now you have got the certificate in john.cer, you can import into the keystore. However, before doing that, you must first import the certificate of the CA itself into your keystore as a trusted CA certficate, otherwise it will refuse to import John's certificate. To do that:

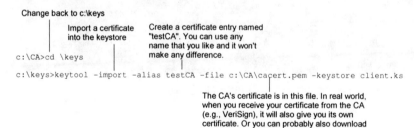

Run it:

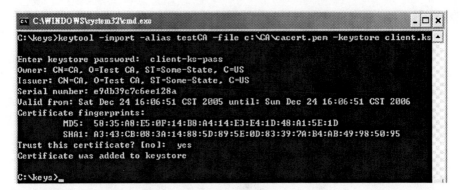

Note that it asked you to trust this certificate or not. This is a very important decision. If you trust this certificate as a CA certificate, you will trust all certificates issued by it. Next, add John's certificate to the keystore to replace his self-signed certificate. This is also done using the -import option:

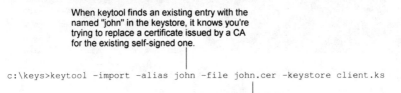

When keytool finds an existing entry with the named "john" in the keystore, it knows you're trying to replace a certificate issued by a CA for the existing self-signed one.

```
c:\keys>keytool -import -alias john -file john.cer -keystore client.ks
```

The certificate is in this file

Run it:

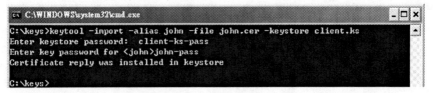

To verify, you can list the entries in the keystore:

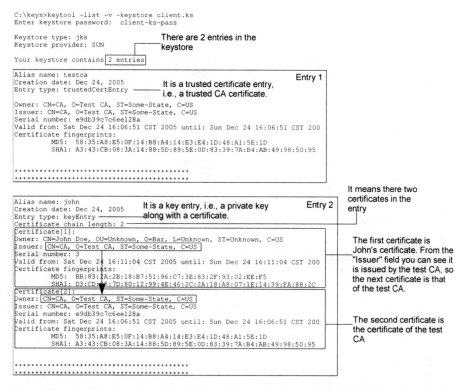

A certificate chain is also called "certificate path". If the certificate of your test CA was issued by yet another CA, then the certificate path would contain the certificate of that other CA as the last certificate.

Signing a SOAP message

Now, let's create a client that signs its messages. First, copy the WrappedService project and paste it as SecureService. Delete the server-config.wsdd file. Rename the word "secure" for "wrapped" in the WSDL file and build.xml. Create a context descriptor SecureService.xml. Generate the service stub and client stub. Fill out the code in the implementation class. Deploy the service.

Next, go to http://ws.apache.org/wss4j to download a library called "WSS4J (Web Service Security for Java)". You will use it to do the signing (and encrypting). Suppose that it is wss4j-bin-1.1.0.zip. Unzip it into say c:\wss4j. You also need to download some 3rd party jar files it needs from the same web page. Suppose that it is wss4j-otherjars-1.1.0.zip. Unzip it into the same folder (c:\wss4j) The jar files will be put into c:\wss4j\lib:

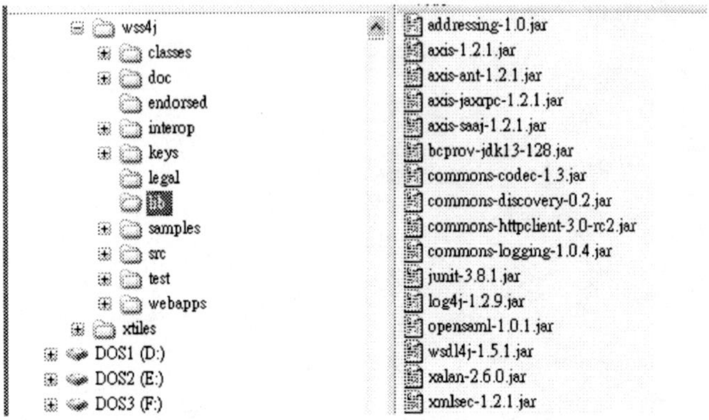

```
⊞ 🗀 wss4j                              📄 addressing-1.0.jar
    ⊞ 🗀 classes                        📄 axis-1.2.1.jar
    ⊞ 🗀 doc                            📄 axis-ant-1.2.1.jar
        🗀 endorsed                     📄 axis-jaxrpc-1.2.1.jar
    ⊞ 🗀 interop                        📄 axis-saaj-1.2.1.jar
    ⊞ 🗀 keys                           📄 bcprov-jdk13-128.jar
        🗀 legal                        📄 commons-codec-1.3.jar
        🗀 lib                          📄 commons-discovery-0.2.jar
    ⊞ 🗀 samples                        📄 commons-httpclient-3.0-rc2.jar
    ⊞ 🗀 src                            📄 commons-logging-1.0.4.jar
    ⊞ 🗀 test                           📄 junit-3.8.1.jar
    ⊞ 🗀 webapps                        📄 log4j-1.2.9.jar
⊞ 🗀 xtiles                             📄 opensaml-1.0.1.jar
⊞ 💾 DOS1 (D:)                          📄 wsdl4j-1.5.1.jar
⊞ 💾 DOS2 (E:)                          📄 xalan-2.6.0.jar
⊞ 💾 DOS3 (F:)                          📄 xmlsec-1.2.1.jar
```

In Eclipse, choose Windows | Preferences, then choose Java | Build Path | User Libraries:

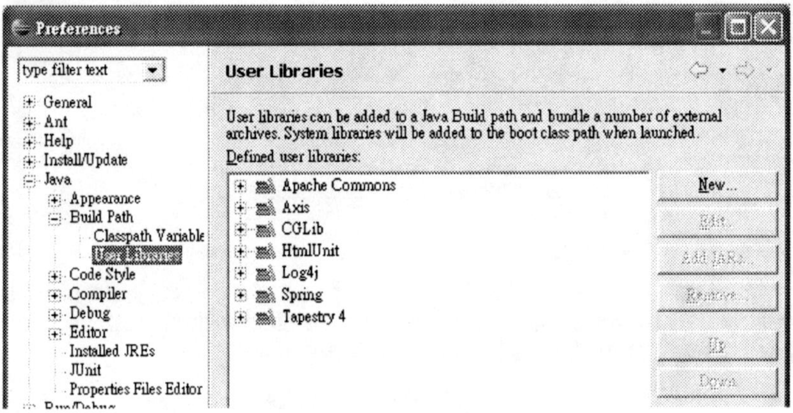

Preferences

| type filter text ▼ | **User Libraries** | ⇦ ▾ ⇨ ▾ |

User libraries can be added to a Java Build path and bundle a number of external archives. System libraries will be added to the boot class path when launched.

Defined user libraries:

- ⊞ General
- ⊞ Ant
- ⊞ Help
- ⊞ Install/Update
- ⊟ Java
  - ⊞ Appearance
  - ⊟ Build Path
    - Classpath Variable
    - **User Libraries**
  - ⊞ Code Style
  - ⊞ Compiler
  - ⊞ Debug
  - ⊞ Editor
  - Installed JREs
  - JUnit
  - Properties Files Editor
  - ⊞ Run/Debug

- ⊞ 📚 Apache Commons
- ⊞ 📚 Axis
- ⊞ 📚 CGLib
- ⊞ 📚 HtmlUnit
- ⊞ 📚 Log4j
- ⊞ 📚 Spring
- ⊞ 📚 Tapestry 4

New...
Edit
Add JARs...
Remove
Up
Down

Click "New" to create a user library named "WSS4J":

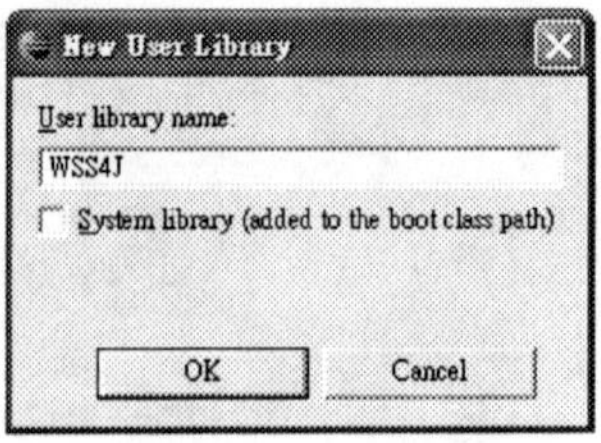

New User Library

User library name:

WSS4J

☐ System library (added to the boot class path)

OK   Cancel

Then click "Add JARs" to add c:\wss4j\wss4j.jar and then some (but NOT all) jar files in c:\wss4j\lib as shown below:

You don't need the other jar files because they're also included in the Axis library. To make them available to the client, right click the SecureService project and choose "Properties", then choose "Java Build Path" and then the "Libraries" tab, add the WSS4J library to it:

To make the jar files available to the service, copy them into c:\workspace\SecureService\context\WEB-INF\lib.   Next,   modify   the DllClient.java in the client package:

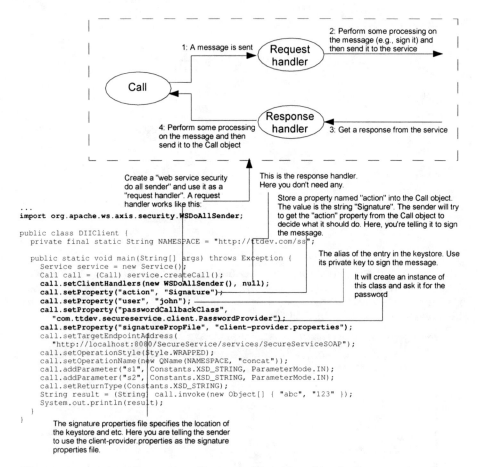

Create a "web service security do all sender" and use it as a "request handler". A request handler works like this:

This is the response handler. Here you don't need any.

Store a property named "action" into the Call object. The value is the string "Signature". The sender will try to get the "action" property from the Call object to decide what it should do. Here, you're telling it to sign the message.

The alias of the entry in the keystore. Use its private key to sign the message.

It will create an instance of this class and ask it for the password

```
...
import org.apache.ws.axis.security.WSDoAllSender;

public class DIIClient {
    private final static String NAMESPACE = "http://ttdev.com/ss";

    public static void main(String[] args) throws Exception {
        Service service = new Service();
        Call call = (Call) service.createCall();
        call.setClientHandlers(new WSDoAllSender(), null);
        call.setProperty("action", "Signature");
        call.setProperty("user", "john");
        call.setProperty("passwordCallbackClass",
            "com.ttdev.secureservice.client.PasswordProvider");
        call.setProperty("signaturePropFile", "client-provider.properties");
        call.setTargetEndpointAddress(
            "http://localhost:8080/SecureService/services/SecureServiceSOAP");
        call.setOperationStyle(Style.WRAPPED);
        call.setOperationName(new QName(NAMESPACE, "concat"));
        call.addParameter("s1", Constants.XSD_STRING, ParameterMode.IN);
        call.addParameter("s2", Constants.XSD_STRING, ParameterMode.IN);
        call.setReturnType(Constants.XSD_STRING);
        String result = (String) call.invoke(new Object[] { "abc", "123" });
        System.out.println(result);
    }
}
```

The signature properties file specifies the location of the keystore and etc. Here you are telling the sender to use the client-provider.properties as the signature properties file.

Of course you need to create a PasswordProvider class in the same package:

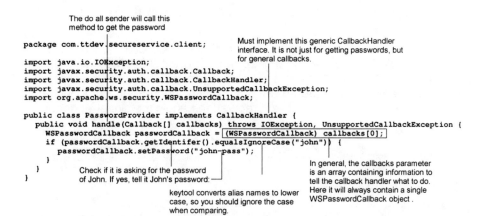

You may wonder why it is so complicated just to tell it the password. Why not just set the password as a property:

```
public class DIIClient {
    private final static String NAMESPACE = "http://ttdev.com/ss";

    public static void main(String[] args) throws Exception {
        Service service = new Service();
        Call call = (Call) service.createCall();
        call.setClientHandlers(new WSDoAllSender(), null);
        call.setProperty("action", "Signature");
        call.setProperty("user", "john");
        call.setProperty("passwordCallbackClass",
            "com.ttdev.secureservice.client.PasswordProvider");
        call.setProperty("password", "john-pass");
        call.setProperty("signaturePropFile", "client-provider.properties");
        call.setTargetEndpointAddress(
            "http://localhost:8080/SecureService/services/SecureServiceSOAP");
        call.setOperationStyle(Style.WRAPPED);
        call.setOperationName(new QName(NAMESPACE, "concat"));
        call.addParameter("s1", Constants.XSD_STRING, ParameterMode.IN);
        call.addParameter("s2", Constants.XSD_STRING, ParameterMode.IN);
        call.setReturnType(Constants.XSD_STRING);
        String result = (String) call.invoke(new Object[] { "abc", "123" });
        System.out.println(result);
    }
}
```

The reason will be explained later. Now, you need to create the client-provider.properties file. Put it into the project root folder and it should be like:

WSS4J use a cryptographic provider to perform signing, encryption and etc. You specify the class of the provider to use this. Here you're telling it to use the Merlin provider which comes with WSS4J and uses the JDK to perform these tasks.

```
org.apache.ws.security.crypto.provider=org.apache.ws.security.components.crypto.Merlin
org.apache.ws.security.crypto.merlin.keystore.password=client-ks-pass
org.apache.ws.security.crypto.merlin.file=c:/keys/client.ks
```

These settings are intended for Merlin only. It has the concept of keystore (a Java concept) and etc.

The path to the keystore

The keystore password

At runtime the do all sender will try to load it from the root of the classpath.

Because you've put it into the project root, it will be copied into the root of the classpath.

Now, deploy the service (which is functionally identical to the original SimpleService). To see the SOAP message, run the TCP Monitor, create a proxy and then configure the client to use that proxy. Finally, run the client and you should see the message in the TCP Monitor (ignore the error printed in the console as the service is not yet prepared to handle the digital signature):

The "mustUnderstand" attribute is set to 1, meaning that the receiver (the service) must handle this header, otherwise it must return a SOAP fault.

A <Security> element is added. It is a header entry.

A <Signature> element represents a digital signature. You don't need to understand its details. If later you encrypt the message, there will be an <EncryptedData> element as its sibling.

```
<soapenv:Envelope
    xmlns:soapenv="http://schemas.xmlsoap.org/soap/envelope/"
    xmlns:xsd="http://www.w3.org/2001/XMLSchema"
    xmlns:xsi="http://www.w3.org/2001/XMLSchema-instance">
    <soapenv:Header>
        <wsse:Security
            xmlns:wsse="http://docs.oasis-open.org/wss/2004/01/oasis-200401-wss-wssecurity-secext-1.0.xsd"
            soapenv:mustUnderstand="1">
            <ds:Signature
                xmlns:ds="http://www.w3.org/2000/09/xmldsig#">
                <ds:SignedInfo>
                    <ds:CanonicalizationMethod Algorithm="http://www.w3.org/2001/10/xml-exc-c14n#"/>
                    <ds:SignatureMethod Algorithm="http://www.w3.org/2000/09/xmldsig#rsa-sha1"/>
                    <ds:Reference URI="#id-19731881">
                        <ds:Transforms>
                            <ds:Transform Algorithm="http://www.w3.org/2001/10/xml-exc-c14n#"/>
                        </ds:Transforms>
                        <ds:DigestMethod Algorithm="http://www.w3.org/2000/09/xmldsig#sha1"/>
                        <ds:DigestValue>noXL+6UoTdGoVd38k9NLXAs8HkA=</ds:DigestValue>
                    </ds:Reference>
                </ds:SignedInfo>
                <ds:SignatureValue>EV0qzgwV5mjaypCEBW/e0e+74dLTFnc...</ds:SignatureValue>
                <ds:KeyInfo Id="KeyId-16607409">
                    <wsse:SecurityTokenReference
                        xmlns:wsu="http://docs.oasis-open.org/wss/2004/01/oasis-200401-wss-wssecurity-utility-1.0.xsd"
                        wsu:Id="STRId-18983808">
                        <ds:X509IssuerSerial>
                            <ds:X509IssuerName>CN=CA,O=Test CA,ST=Some-State,C=US</ds:X509IssuerName>
                            <ds:X509SerialNumber>3</ds:X509SerialNumber>
                        </ds:X509IssuerSerial>
                    </wsse:SecurityTokenReference>
                </ds:KeyInfo>
            </ds:Signature>
        </wsse:Security>
    </soapenv:Header>
    <soapenv:Body
        xmlns:wsu="http://docs.oasis-open.org/wss/2004/01/oasis-200401-wss-wssecurity-utility-1.0.xsd"
        wsu:Id="id-19731881">
        <concat xmlns="http://ttdev.com/ss">
            <s1 xmlns="" xsi:type="xsd:string">abc</s1>
            <s2 xmlns="" xsi:type="xsd:string">123</s2>
        </concat>
    </soapenv:Body>
</soapenv:Envelope>
```

The signature is signing over this element, i.e., the <Body> element.

The <Body> element is basically unchanged. The only exception is that an id has been added so that the signature can refer to it.

Another point to note is:

```
...
<ds:Signature xmlns:ds="http://www.w3.org/2000/09/xmldsig#">
    ...
    <ds:KeyInfo Id="KeyId-13626440">
        <wsse:SecurityTokenReference
            xmlns:wsu="http://docs.oasis-open.org/wss/2004/01/oasis-200401-wss-
wssecurity-utility-1.0.xsd"
            wsu:Id="STRId-10690075">
            <ds:X509IssuerSerial>
                <ds:X509IssuerName>
                    CN=CA,O=Test CA,ST=Some-State,C=US
                </ds:X509IssuerName>
                <ds:X509SerialNumber>3</ds:X509SerialNumber>
            </ds:X509IssuerSerial>
        </wsse:SecurityTokenReference>
    </ds:KeyInfo>
```

```
</ds:Signature>
```
That is, it is telling the service that the certificate used to sign the message is issued by CN=CA,O=Test CA,ST=Some-State,C=US and the serial number of the certificate is 3. It is hoping that the service can use this information to locate the certificate and then use the public key in it to verify the signature. For this to work, the service may scan all the certificates in the keystore to try to find it. It means you must import John's certificate into the keystore on the server. If this is too much trouble, you can tell the do all sender to include John's certificate into the message itself:

```
public class DIIClient {
  private final static String NAMESPACE = "http://ttdev.com/ss";

  public static void main(String[] args) throws Exception {
    Service service = new Service();
    Call call = (Call) service.createCall();
    call.setClientHandlers(new WSDoAllSender(), null);
    call.setProperty("action", "Signature");
    call.setProperty("user", "john");
    call.setProperty("passwordCallbackClass",
      "com.ttdev.secureservice.client.PasswordProvider");
    call.setProperty("signaturePropFile", "client-provider.properties");
    call.setProperty("signatureKeyIdentifier", "DirectReference");
    call.setTargetEndpointAddress(
      "http://localhost:8080/SecureService/services/SecureServiceSOAP");
    call.setOperationStyle(Style.WRAPPED);
    call.setOperationName(new QName(NAMESPACE, "concat"));
    call.addParameter("s1", Constants.XSD_STRING, ParameterMode.IN);
    call.addParameter("s2", Constants.XSD_STRING, ParameterMode.IN);
    call.setReturnType(Constants.XSD_STRING);
    String result = (String) call.invoke(new Object[] { "abc", "123" });
    System.out.println(result);
  }
}
```

Making it optional

As the service is not understanding the digital signature yet, it is not running. Is it possible to set mustUnderstand to 0? Yes, just do it like this:

```
public class DIIClient {
  private final static String NAMESPACE = "http://ttdev.com/ss";

  public static void main(String[] args) throws Exception {
    Service service = new Service();
    Call call = (Call) service.createCall();
    call.setClientHandlers(new WSDoAllSender(), null);
    call.setProperty("action", "Signature");
    call.setProperty("user", "john");
    call.setProperty("passwordCallbackClass",
      "com.ttdev.secureservice.client.PasswordProvider");
    call.setProperty("signaturePropFile", "client-provider.properties");
    call.setProperty("signatureKeyIdentifier", "DirectReference");
    call.setProperty("mustUnderstand", "0");
    call.setTargetEndpointAddress(
      "http://localhost:8080/SecureService/services/SecureServiceSOAP");
    call.setOperationStyle(Style.WRAPPED);
    call.setOperationName(new QName(NAMESPACE, "concat"));
    call.addParameter("s1", Constants.XSD_STRING, ParameterMode.IN);
    call.addParameter("s2", Constants.XSD_STRING, ParameterMode.IN);
    call.setReturnType(Constants.XSD_STRING);
    String result = (String) call.invoke(new Object[] { "abc", "123" });
    System.out.println(result);
  }
}
```

Then run it and it will work:

```
Console ✕    Problems  Javadoc  Declaration  SVN Repository  Console  Search
<terminated> SecureClient [Java Application] C:\Program Files\Java\jre1.5.0_02\bin\javaw.exe (Dec 22, 2005 5:54:28 PM)
- Using Crypto Engine [org.apache.ws.security.components.crypto.Merlin]
abc123
```

For better security, let's remove this line to force the service to handle it.

Using symbolic constants

It is easy to have typos in the property names. Therefore, WSS4J has defined symbolic constants for them for you to use:

```
public static void main(String[] args) throws Exception {
  Service service = new Service();
  Call call = (Call) service.createCall();
  call.setClientHandlers(new WSDoAllSender(), null);
  call.setProperty(WSHandlerConstants.ACTION, "Signature");
  call.setProperty(WSHandlerConstants.USER, "john");
  call.setProperty(WSHandlerConstants.PW_CALLBACK_CLASS,
    "com.ttdev.secureservice.client.PasswordProvider");
  call.setProperty(WSHandlerConstants.SIG_PROP_FILE,
    "client-provider.properties");
  call.setProperty(WSHandlerConstants.SIG_KEY_ID, "DirectReference");
  ...
}
```

Run it and it will continue to work.

Verifying the digital signature

To verify the digital signature, the service can use a request handler:

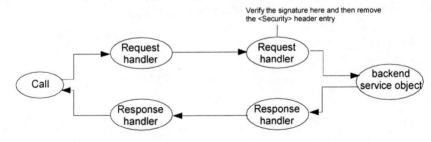

To do that, modify deploy.wsdd:

Annotations:

- You can use anything as the name of the handler
- It is a QName. The namespace is the java namespace.
- This is NOT to tell it to verify the signature. It is telling it to process the message only if it has been signed. Otherwise treat it as an error. That is, this is a security check, not an action.
- Tell it to use the service-provider.properties file as the signature properties file
- Use the "do all receiver" as the handler. It can verify a signature and decrypt SOAP messages.

```xml
<deployment
  xmlns="http://xml.apache.org/axis/wsdd/"
  xmlns:java="http://xml.apache.org/axis/wsdd/providers/java">
<handler name="receiver" type="java:org.apache.ws.axis.security.WSDoAllReceiver">
  <parameter name="action" value="Signature"/>
  <parameter name="signaturePropFile" value="service-provider.properties"/>
</handler>
  <service name="SecureServiceSOAP" provider="java:RPC" style="wrapped" use="literal">
    <parameter name="wsdlTargetNamespace" value="http://ttdev.com/ss"/>
    <parameter name="wsdlServiceElement" value="SecureService"/>
    <parameter name="schemaUnqualified" value="http://ttdev.com/ss"/>
    <parameter name="wsdlServicePort" value="SecureServiceSOAP"/>
    <parameter name="className" value="com.ttdev.secureservice.SecureServiceSOAPImpl"/>
    <parameter name="wsdlPortType" value="SecureService"/>
    <parameter name="typeMappingVersion" value="1.2"/>
    <operation name="concat"
      qname="operNS:concat"
      xmlns:operNS="http://ttdev.com/ss"
      returnQName="concatResponse" returnType="rtns:string"
      xmlns:rtns="http://www.w3.org/2001/XMLSchema"
      soapAction="http://ttdev.com/ss/NewOperation" >
      <parameter qname="s1" type="tns:string" xmlns:tns="http://www.w3.org/2001/XMLSchema"/>
      <parameter qname="s2" type="tns:string" xmlns:tns="http://www.w3.org/2001/XMLSchema"/>
    </operation>
    <parameter name="allowedMethods" value="concat"/>
    <requestFlow>
      <handler type="receiver"/>
    </requestFlow>
  </service>
</deployment>
```

You can put one or more handlers into a <requestFlow>. They will each get a chance to process the request for this service.

Create the service-provider.properties file in the project root folder so that it will be put into the root of the classpath (WEB-INF/classes):

```
org.apache.ws.security.crypto.provider=org.apache.ws.security.components.crypto.
Merlin
org.apache.ws.security.crypto.merlin.keystore.password=service-ks-pass
org.apache.ws.security.crypto.merlin.file=c:/keys/service.ks
```

You need to create the service.ks keystore, use "service-ks-pass" as the keystore password and import the certificate of the test CA into there:

```
C:\WINDOWS\system32\cmd.exe                                          _ □ x

C:\keys>keytool -import -alias testCA -file c:\CA\cacert.pem -keystore service.k
s
Enter keystore password: service-ks-pass
Owner: CN=CA, O=Test CA, ST=Some-State, C=US
Issuer: CN=CA, O=Test CA, ST=Some-State, C=US
Serial number: e9db39c7c6ee128a
Valid from: Sat Dec 24 16:06:51 CST 2005 until: Sun Dec 24 16:06:51 CST 2006
Certificate fingerprints:
         MD5:  58:35:A8:E5:0F:14:B8:A4:14:E3:E4:1D:48:A1:5E:1D
         SHA1: A3:43:CB:08:3A:14:88:5D:89:5E:0D:83:39:7A:B4:AB:49:98:50:95
Trust this certificate? [no]: yes
Certificate was added to keystore

C:\keys>
```

Note that you don't need the import John's certificate as it will be included in the message. Now, deploy the service again so that the handler is installed. Now, run the client and it should work:

```
Console  ✕    Problems  Javadoc  Declaration  SVN Repository  Console  Search
<terminated> SecureClient [Java Application] C:\Program Files\Java\jre1.5.0_02\bin\javaw.exe (Dec 22, 2005 7:59:08 PM)
- Using Crypto Engine [org.apache.ws.security.components.crypto.Merlin]
abc123
```

Prompting for the password

For the moment the password provider is just returning a hard code password "john-pass". In real life, it may prompt the user for the password, query a database and etc. Suppose that you'd like to prompt the user. In addition, you'd like to print a prompt telling the user what it is trying to do to justify why it needs his password, such as "You're trying to sign a message to concatenate abc and 123 as John, please enter your password". To do that, modify DIIClient.java:

```java
public class DIIClient {
    private final static String NAMESPACE = "http://ttdev.com/ss";

    public static void main(String[] args) throws Exception {
        Service service = new Service();
        Call call = (Call) service.createCall();
        call.setClientHandlers(new WSDoAllSender(), null);
        call.setProperty(WSHandlerConstants.ACTION, "Signature");
        call.setProperty(WSHandlerConstants.USER, "john");
        call.setProperty(WSHandlerConstants.PW_CALLBACK_CLASS,
            "com.ttdev.secureservice.client.PasswordPrompter");
        call.setProperty(WSHandlerConstants.SIG_PROP_FILE,
            "client-provider.properties");
        call.setProperty(WSHandlerConstants.SIG_KEY_ID, "DirectReference");
        call.setProperty("taskDescription", "concatenate abc and 123");
        call.setTargetEndpointAddress(
            "http://localhost:8080/SecureService/services/SecureServiceSOAP");
        call.setOperationStyle(Style.WRAPPED);
        call.setOperationName(new QName(NAMESPACE, "concat"));
        call.addParameter("s1", Constants.XSD_STRING, ParameterMode.IN);
        call.addParameter("s2", Constants.XSD_STRING, ParameterMode.IN);
        call.setReturnType(Constants.XSD_STRING);
        String result = (String) call.invoke(new Object[] { "abc", "123" });
        System.out.println(result);
    }
}
```

You'll create this PasswordPrompter class to prompt for the password

Store the task description as a property of the Call object. Later the PasswordPrompter should retrieve it.

Create PasswordPrompter.java in the com.ttdev.secureservice.client package:

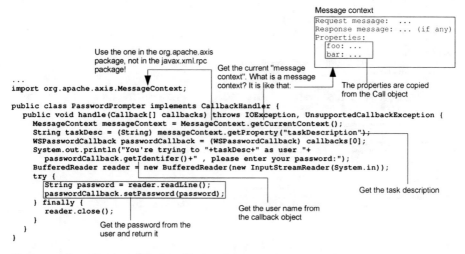

Now, run the client and it should prompt you:

```
Console  ×  Problems  Javadoc  Declaration  SVN Repository  Console  Search
<terminated> SecureClient [Java Application] C:\Program Files\Java\jre1.5.0_02\bin\javaw.exe (Dec 24, 2005 4:33:07 PM)
- Using Crypto Engine [org.apache.ws.security.components.crypto.Merlin]
You're trying to concatenate abc and 123 as user john , please enter your password:
john-pass
abc123
```

Performing configurations at deployment time

So it's working fine. But if your client is using a stub? Create a StubClient.java in the client package:

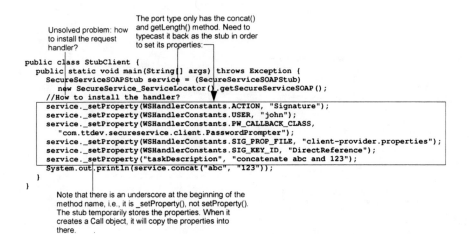

As you can see, there is no Call object in the code at all. It will be created by the stub when you call a business method like concat(). Therefore you can't call setClientHandlers() on the Call object. To solve the problem, you need to understand how the message flows in the client. For example (see the diagram below), after a message is created, if it is calling the port named "Foo", then you can configure a request flow for those messages calling the port named "Foo" and put one or more handlers in the flow. This way, that message will go through the handlers. Then, Axis will look at the endpoint of the message. In particular, it looks at the scheme (http as in http://...) and use it to lookup a "transport object" with this name and then ask it to send the message to the network. Axis by default has such a transport object and some others (e.g., one for https). When the transport object receives the response message, it will forward it back to the response flow and finally the message will get back to the caller:

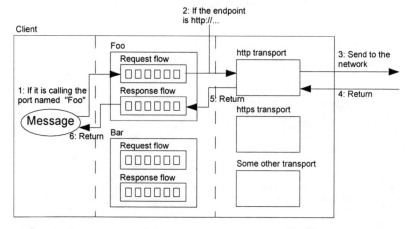

To configure the request flow, create a file named client-config.wsdd (the name is important) in the project root folder so that it will go into the classpath root. It should be like:

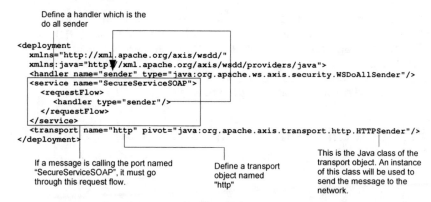

Why do you need to define the "http" transport object again? It should be defined by Axis, right? This is because if there is no client-config.wsdd file, Axis will use a default version coming with Axis. The default version already defines the http transport so it has been working fine. But now as you have your own configuration file, you must define it otherwise you will get an error saying there is no transport named "http". Anyway, now run the StubClient and it will work.

If you'd like, you can set the properties of the handler in the client-config.wsdd:

```
<deployment
  xmlns="http://xml.apache.org/axis/wsdd/"
  xmlns:java="http://xml.apache.org/axis/wsdd/providers/java">
  <handler name="sender" type="java:org.apache.ws.axis.security.WSDoAllSender">
    <parameter name="action" value="signature"/>
    <parameter name="signaturePropFile" value="client-provider.properties"/>
    <parameter name="signatureKeyIdentifier" value="DirectReference"/>
    <parameter name="user" value="john"/>
    <parameter name="passwordCallbackClass"
```

```
    value="com.ttdev.secureservice.client.PasswordPrompter"/>
  </handler>
  <service name="SecureServiceSOAP">
    <requestFlow>
      <handler type="sender"/>
    </requestFlow>
  </service>
  <transport name="http"
    pivot="java:org.apache.axis.transport.http.HTTPSender"/>
</deployment>
```

Then you don't need to do that in Java code (even if you do, they will be overridden by the configuration file):

```
public class StubClient {
  public static void main(String[] args) throws Exception {
    SecureServiceSOAPStub service = (SecureServiceSOAPStub)
      new SecureService_ServiceLocator().getSecureServiceSOAP();
    service._setProperty(WSHandlerConstants.ACTION, "Signature");
    service._setProperty(WSHandlerConstants.USER, "john");
    service._setProperty(WSHandlerConstants.PW_CALLBACK_CLASS,
      "com.ttdev.secureservice.client.PasswordPrompter");
    service._setProperty(WSHandlerConstants.SIG_PROP_FILE,
      "client provider.properties");
    service._setProperty(WSHandlerConstants.SIG_KEY_ID, "DirectReference");
    service._setProperty("taskDescription", "concatenate abc and 123");
    System.out.println(service.concat("abc", "123"));
  }
}
```

Run it and it should continue to work. You may wonder why do that? As the developer of the web service, you may not know everything, e.g., how to secure the message (sign, encrypt or both?), what user name to use, how to provide the password and etc. Therefore, it makes sense to let the person deploying the web service to decide. Then he can create his client-config.wsdd and put it into the classpath root.

Letting the DII client use the client-config.wsdd file

Can the DII client use the client-config.wsdd file? Let's delete the following code:

```
public class DIIClient {
  private final static String NAMESPACE = "http://ttdev.com/ss";

  public static void main(String[] args) throws Exception {
    Service service = new Service();
    Call call = (Call) service.createCall();
    call.setClientHandlers(new WSDoAllSender(), null);
    call.setProperty(WSHandlerConstants.ACTION, "Signature");
    call.setProperty(WSHandlerConstants.USER, "john");
    call.setProperty(WSHandlerConstants.PW_CALLBACK_CLASS,
      "com.ttdev.secureservice.client.PasswordPrompter");
    call.setProperty(WSHandlerConstants.SIG_PROP_FILE,
      "client provider.properties");
    call.setProperty(WSHandlerConstants.SIG_KEY_ID, "DirectReference");
    call.setProperty("taskDescription", "concatenate abc and 123");
    call.setTargetEndpointAddress(
      "http://localhost:8080/SecureService/services/SecureServiceSOAP");
    call.setOperationStyle(Style.WRAPPED);
    call.setOperationName(new QName(NAMESPACE, "concat"));
    call.addParameter("s1", Constants.XSD_STRING, ParameterMode.IN);
    call.addParameter("s2", Constants.XSD_STRING, ParameterMode.IN);
    call.setReturnType(Constants.XSD_STRING);
    String result = (String) call.invoke(new Object[] { "abc", "123" });
    System.out.println(result);
```

```
      }
   }
```

Run it and it will fail:

```
⊟ Console ✕    Problems  Javadoc  Declaration  SVN Repository  Console  Search              ⊠ ✖  ⊡ ⊡  ⌁
<terminated> SecureClient [Java Application] C:\Program Files\Java\jre1.5.0_02\bin\javaw.exe (Dec 24, 2005 11:24:16 AM)
Exception in thread "main" AxisFault
   faultCode: {http://schemas.xmlsoap.org/soap/envelope/}Server.generalException
   faultSubcode:
   faultString: WSDoAllReceiver: Request does not contain required Security header
```

This is because this Call object doesn't know the port name it is calling and
therefore the request flow you defined above is not applied to the message.
To solve the problem, just tell it the port name:

```
public class DIIClient {
   private final static String NAMESPACE = "http://ttdev.com/ss";

   public static void main(String[] args) throws Exception {
      Service service = new Service();
      Call call = (Call) service.createCall();
      call.setPortName(new QName(NAMESPACE, "SecureServiceSOAP"));
      call.setProperty("taskDescription", "concatenate abc and 123");
      call.setTargetEndpointAddress(
         "http://localhost:8080/SecureService/services/SecureServiceSOAP");
      call.setOperationStyle(Style.WRAPPED);
      call.setOperationName(new QName(NAMESPACE, "concat"));
      call.addParameter("s1", Constants.XSD_STRING, ParameterMode.IN);
      call.addParameter("s2", Constants.XSD_STRING, ParameterMode.IN);
      call.setReturnType(Constants.XSD_STRING);
      String result = (String) call.invoke(new Object[] { "abc", "123" });
      System.out.println(result);
   }
}
```

Even though you need to pass it a QName, only the local name is used. Now,
run it and it should work.

Retrieving the user information in the back end object

Suppose that you'd like to allow certain people only to call your service.
However, the receive all handler can only check if the request message claims
it is signed by John, then it is indeed signed by John (see the diagram below).
As long as the claim is true (i.e., the signature can be verified), it will forward it
to the back end object for processing. It will not know say only John is allowed
to use that service but not Paul:

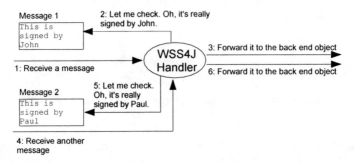

Only your back end service can make that decision. To do that, it will need to find out the user's (verified) DN. How? You need to first understand how a WSS4J handler reports its result. A WSS4J handler may be asked to perform multiple actions (see the diagram below), e.g., decrypt a message and then verify its signature. After performing these actions, it will create a WSHandlerResult to report its result. This WSHandlerResult is basically a Vector. Each element of the Vector is a WSSecurityEngineResult, which is just the result of each action performed. For example, for a signature action (verify signature), the result contains the action ("Sign"), the certificate used and etc. For an encryption action (decrypt message), the result contains the action ("Encrypt"). In order to pass the WSHandlerResult to the back end object, it would like to store it into a property. However, it is possible that there are some other WSS4J handlers in the request flow, so it creates a Vector and put its result into there and store the Vector into a property. This way, the subsequent WSS4J handlers can accumulate their results into that Vector:

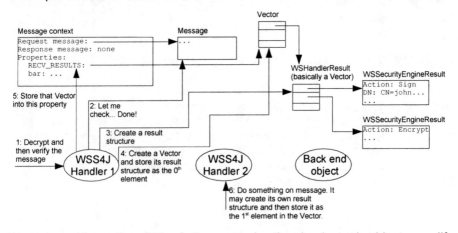

Now, to retrieve the DN of the user in the back end object, modify SecureService.java:

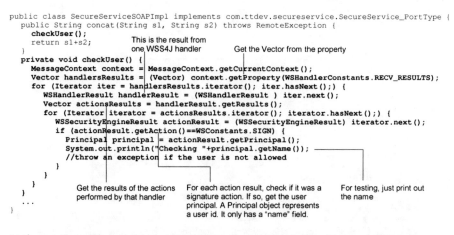

```
public class SecureServiceSOAPImpl implements com.ttdev.secureservice.SecureService_PortType {
    public String concat(String s1, String s2) throws RemoteException {
        checkUser();
        return s1+s2;                    This is the result from
    }                                    one WSS4J handler        Get the Vector from the property
    private void checkUser() {
        MessageContext context = MessageContext.getCurrentContext();
        Vector handlersResults = (Vector) context.getProperty(WSHandlerConstants.RECV_RESULTS);
        for (Iterator iter = handlersResults.iterator(); iter.hasNext();) {
            WSHandlerResult handlerResult = (WSHandlerResult ) iter.next();
            Vector actionsResults = handlerResult.getResults();
            for (Iterator iterator = actionsResults.iterator(); iterator.hasNext();) {
                WSSecurityEngineResult actionResult = (WSSecurityEngineResult) iterator.next();
                if (actionResult.getAction()==WSConstants.SIGN) {
                    Principal principal = actionResult.getPrincipal();
                    System.out.println("Checking "+principal.getName());
                    //throw an exception if the user is not allowed
                }
            }
        }
    }
    ...
}
```

| Get the results of the actions performed by that handler | For each action result, check if it was a signature action. If so, get the user principal. A Principal object represents a user id. It only has a "name" field. | For testing, just print out the name |

Now run the client and you should see the output in the Tomcat console:

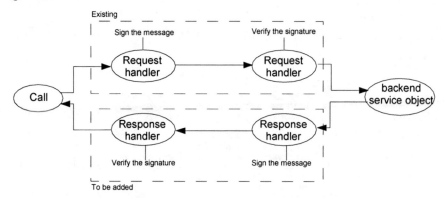

```
Dec 24, 2005 11:59:51 AM org.apache.catalina.core.StandardContext reload
INFO: Reloading this Context has started
- Using Crypto Engine [org.apache.ws.security.components.crypto.Merlin]
- Verification successful for URI "#id-22676229"
Checking CN=John Doe, OU=Unknown, O=Bar, L=Unknown, ST=Unknown, C=US
```

Signing the response message

At the moment only the request message is signed, but the response message is not. This is insecure. To sign the response, you need to get a certificate for the service, install a response handler for the back end object to sign the response and install a response handler on the client to verify the signature:

```
Existing
        Sign the message              Verify the signature
       ┌──────────┐                  ┌──────────┐
       │ Request  │ ───────────────▶ │ Request  │
       │ handler  │                  │ handler  │        ┌──────────┐
       └──────────┘                  └──────────┘───────▶│ backend  │
  ┌──────┐                                                │ service  │
  │ Call │                                                │  object  │
  └──────┘                                                └──────────┘
       ┌──────────┐                  ┌──────────┐
       │ Response │ ◀─────────────── │ Response │◀───────
       │ handler  │                  │ handler  │
       └──────────┘                  └──────────┘
    Verify the signature              Sign the message
    To be added
```

To get a certificate for the service, open a command prompt and then:

```
c:\>cd \keys

c:\keys>keytool -genkey -alias SecureService -keystore service.ks -keyalg RSA
-sigalg SHA1withRSA
```

```
Enter keystore password:  service-ks-pass
What is your first and last name?
  [Unknown]:  SecureService
What is the name of your organizational unit?
  [Unknown]:
What is the name of your organization?
  [Unknown]:  Foo
What is the name of your City or Locality?
  [Unknown]:
What is the name of your State or Province?
  [Unknown]:
What is the two-letter country code for this unit?
  [Unknown]:  US
Is CN=SecureService, OU=Unknown, O=Foo, L=Unknown, ST=Unknown, C=US correct?
  [no]:  yes
Enter key password for <SecureService>
          (RETURN if same as keystore password):  SecureService-pass
```

Generate a certificate request for it:

```
c:\keys>keytool -certreq -alias SecureService -keystore service.ks -file
SecureService.csr
Enter keystore password:  service-ks-pass
Enter key password for <SecureService>SecureService-pass
```

Use your test CA to create a certificate for it (remember that "ca-pass" is the password for the CA key):

```
c:\keys>cd \CA

c:\CA>openssl x509 -CA cacert.pem -CAkey cakey.pem -CAserial serial.txt -req -in
c:\keys\SecureService.csr -out c:\keys\SecureService.cer -days 365
```

Import the certificate into the keystore for the service:

```
c:\CA>cd \keys

c:\keys>keytool -import -alias SecureService -keystore service.ks -file
SecureService.cer
Enter keystore password:  service-ks-pass
Enter key password for <SecureService>SecureService-pass
Certificate reply was installed in keystore
```

Import it into the keystore for the client:

```
c:\keys>keytool -import -alias SecureService -keystore client.ks -file
SecureService.cer
Enter keystore password:  client-ks-pass
Certificate was added to keystore
```

Install the response handler in deploy.wsdd:

```xml
<deployment
  xmlns="http://xml.apache.org/axis/wsdd/"
  xmlns:java="http://xml.apache.org/axis/wsdd/providers/java">
  <handler name="receiver"
    type="java:org.apache.ws.axis.security.WSDoAllReceiver">
    <parameter name="action" value="Signature"/>
    <parameter name="signaturePropFile" value="service-provider.properties"/>
  </handler>
  <handler name="sender" type="java:org.apache.ws.axis.security.WSDoAllSender">
    <parameter name="action" value="Signature"/>
    <parameter name="signaturePropFile" value="service-provider.properties"/>
    <parameter name="signatureKeyIdentifier" value="DirectReference"/>
    <parameter name="user" value="SecureService"/>
    <parameter name="passwordCallbackClass"
      value="com.ttdev.secureservice.PasswordProvider"/>
  </handler>
  <service name="SecureServiceSOAP" provider="java:RPC"
    style="wrapped" use="literal">
    <requestFlow>
      <handler type="receiver"/>
    </requestFlow>
    <responseFlow>
```

```
        <handler type="sender"/>
    </responseFlow>
        ...
    </service>
</deployment>
```

Create PasswordProvider.java in the com.ttdev.secureservice package:

```java
public class PasswordProvider implements CallbackHandler {
    public void handle(Callback[] callbacks)
        throws IOException, UnsupportedCallbackException {
        WSPasswordCallback passwordCallback = (WSPasswordCallback) callbacks[0];
        if (passwordCallback.getIdentifer().equalsIgnoreCase("SecureService")) {
            passwordCallback.setPassword("SecureService-pass");
        }
    }
}
```

Deploy the service again so that the changes take effect. To install the response handler on the client, modify client-config.wsdd:

```xml
<deployment
  xmlns="http://xml.apache.org/axis/wsdd/"
  xmlns:java="http://xml.apache.org/axis/wsdd/providers/java">
  <handler name="sender" type="java:org.apache.ws.axis.security.WSDoAllSender">
    <parameter name="action" value="Signature"/>
    <parameter name="signaturePropFile" value="client-provider.properties"/>
    <parameter name="signatureKeyIdentifier" value="DirectReference"/>
    <parameter name="user" value="john"/>
    <parameter name="passwordCallbackClass"
      value="com.ttdev.secureservice.client.PasswordPrompter"/>
  </handler>
  <handler name="receiver"
    type="java:org.apache.ws.axis.security.WSDoAllReceiver">
    <parameter name="action" value="Signature"/>
    <parameter name="signaturePropFile" value="client-provider.properties"/>
  </handler>
  <service name="SecureServiceSOAP">
    <requestFlow>
      <handler type="sender"/>
    </requestFlow>
    <responseFlow>
      <handler type="receiver"/>
    </responseFlow>
  </service>
  <transport name="http"
    pivot="java:org.apache.axis.transport.http.HTTPSender"/>
</deployment>
```

Run the client and it should work. To be sure the response is indeed signed, use the TCP Monitor:

Encrypting the request message

At the moment the request message is signed, but it is not encrypted and thus people on the Internet can see it. If the information is confidential, you should encrypt it. To do that, modify client-config.wsdd:

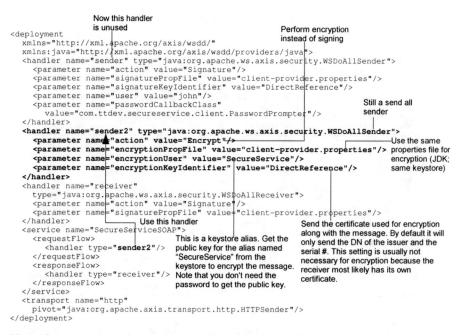

```
<deployment
    xmlns="http://xml.apache.org/axis/wsdd/"
    xmlns:java="http://xml.apache.org/axis/wsdd/providers/java">
    <handler name="sender" type="java:org.apache.ws.axis.security.WSDoAllSender">
        <parameter name="action" value="Signature"/>
        <parameter name="signaturePropFile" value="client-provider.properties"/>
        <parameter name="signatureKeyIdentifier" value="DirectReference"/>
        <parameter name="user" value="john"/>
        <parameter name="passwordCallbackClass"
            value="com.ttdev.secureservice.client.PasswordPrompter"/>
    </handler>
    <handler name="sender2" type="java:org.apache.ws.axis.security.WSDoAllSender">
        <parameter name="action" value="Encrypt"/>
        <parameter name="encryptionPropFile" value="client-provider.properties"/>
        <parameter name="encryptionUser" value="SecureService"/>
        <parameter name="encryptionKeyIdentifier" value="DirectReference"/>
    </handler>
    <handler name="receiver"
        type="java:org.apache.ws.axis.security.WSDoAllReceiver">
        <parameter name="action" value="Signature"/>
        <parameter name="signaturePropFile" value="client-provider.properties"/>
    </handler>
    <service name="SecureServiceSOAP">
        <requestFlow>
            <handler type="sender2"/>
        </requestFlow>
        <responseFlow>
            <handler type="receiver"/>
        </responseFlow>
    </service>
    <transport name="http"
        pivot="java:org.apache.axis.transport.http.HTTPSender"/>
</deployment>
```

Now the message is encrypted (but not signed). As it needs to use the certificate of the service to encrypt the message, you need to have it in the client keystore. Do you have it? Yes! You have imported the certificate of the service into the client keystore when you needed to verify the signature in the response from the service.

For the service to decrypt the message, it also needs a handler. Modify deploy.wsdd:

```
                        Now this handler      Process the message only if it has
                        is unused             been encrypted                                Still a do all
<deployment                                                                                 receiver
   xmlns="http://xml.apache.org/axis/wsdd/"
   xmlns:java="http://xml.apache.org/axis/wsdd/providers/java">
   <handler name="receiver" type="java:org.apache.ws.axis.security.WSDoAllReceiver">
     <parameter name="action" value="Signature"/>
     <parameter name="signaturePropFile" value="service-provider.properties"/>
   </handler>
   <handler name="receiver2" type="java:org.apache.ws.axis.security.WSDoAllReceiver">
     <parameter name="action" value="Encrypt"/>
     <parameter name="decryptionPropFile" value="service-provider.properties"/>
     <parameter name="passwordCallbackClass"
       value="com.ttdev.secureservice.PasswordProvider"/>             Use the same properties
   </handler>                                                          file as for signature
   <handler name="sender" type="java:org.apache.ws.axis.security.WSDoAllSender">  verification
     <parameter name="action" value="Signature"/>
     <parameter name="signaturePropFile" value="service-provider.properties"/>
     <parameter name="signatureKeyIdentifier" value="DirectReference"/>
     <parameter name="user" value="SecureService"/>
     <parameter name="passwordCallbackClass"
       value="com.ttdev.secureservice.PasswordProvider"/>
   </handler>
   <service name="SecureServiceSOAP" provider="java:RPC" style="wrapped" use="literal">
     <requestFlow>
       <handler type="receiver2"/>            Use this handler
     </requestFlow>
     <responseFlow>
       <handler type="sender"/>                      To decrypt the message, it will get the
     </responseFlow>                                 certificate from the message, find a key entry in
     ...                                             the keystore that contains this certificate. Then
   </service>                                        to get the private key of that entry, it will call this
</deployment>                                        password callback handler and pass the alias
                                                     name to it.

                            This is why it needs to use a callback handler. You just can't give
                            it a password beforehand. This is true for the receiver. For the
                            sender, this is not the case, but the developer of WSS4J decided
                            to use the same mechanism for both the sender and the receiver.
                            So you end up having to use a callback handler to set the
                            password.
```

Deploy the service again. Now run the client and it should work. If you watch the messages in TCP Monitor, you'll find that the request is indeed encrypted:

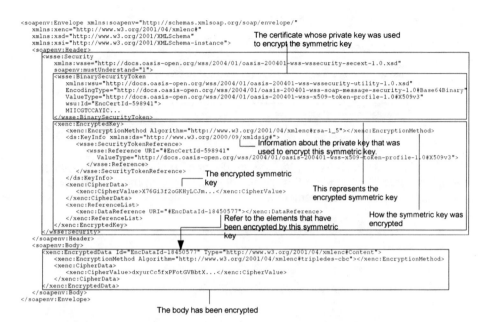

The body has been encrypted

Removing dangling references to resources

Once you're using encryption, you may notice that whenever your web application is reloaded, it may die with a ThreadDeath exception. This is because the encryption library (called "bouncy castle") is hanging onto some resources that have been released. To solve the problem, you should remove the references when your application is shutdown. To do that, modify c:\workspace\SecureService\context\WEB-INF\web.xml:

```
<web-app>
    <display-name>Apache-Axis</display-name>
    <listener>
        <listener-class>org.apache.axis.transport.http.AxisHTTPSessionListener</listener-class>
    </listener>
    <listener>
        <listener-class>com.ttdev.secureservice.CleanupListener</listener-class>
    </listener>
    ...
</web-app>
```

Call this listener when the web application is shutdown. You will need to create this class.

Create CleanupListener.java in the com.ttdev.secureservice package:

```
. . .
import java.beans.Introspector;
import javax.servlet.ServletContextEvent;
import javax.servlet.ServletContextListener;    Must implement this interface
import org.apache.log4j.LogManager;

public class CleanupListener implements ServletContextListener {
    public void contextInitialized(ServletContextEvent arg0) {
    }
    public void contextDestroyed(ServletContextEvent arg0) {
        LogManager.shutdown();  ———————— Shutdown the logging library
        Introspector.flushCaches();    used by Axis
    }
}
                        Cleanup the "introspector"
                        used by bouncy castle library
```

The ServletContextListener interface is defined in the servlet specification (servlet-api.jar). You can find this jar file in c:\tomcat\common\lib. So, add it to the Java build path of your project:

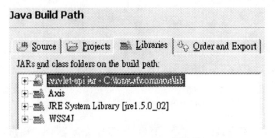

Now, reload the web application for it to take effect.

Combining signing and encrypting

At the moment the request message is encrypted but not signed. How to perform both? Just merge the two senders in client-config.wsdd:

Encrypt and then sign. Why not sign and then encrypt?

The parameters of the original sender2

```
<deployment
   xmlns="http://xml.apache.org/axis/wsdd/"
   xmlns:java="http://xml.apache.org/axis/wsdd/providers/java">
   <handler name="sender" type="java:org.apache.ws.axis.security.WSDoAllSender">
      <parameter name="action" value="Encrypt Signature"/>
      <parameter name="signaturePropFile" value="client-provider.properties"/>
      <parameter name="signatureKeyIdentifier" value="DirectReference"/>
      <parameter name="user" value="john"/>
      <parameter name="passwordCallbackClass"
         value="com.ttdev.secureservice.client.PasswordPrompter"/>
      <parameter name="encryptionPropFile" value="client-provider.properties"/>
      <parameter name="encryptionUser" value="SecureService"/>
      <parameter name="encryptionKeyIdentifier" value="DirectReference"/>
   </handler>
   <handler name="receiver"
      type="java:org.apache.ws.axis.security.WSDoAllReceiver">
      <parameter name="action" value="Signature"/>
      <parameter name="signaturePropFile" value="client-provider.properties"/>
   </handler>
   <service name="SecureServiceSOAP">
      <requestFlow>
         <handler type="sender"/>
      </requestFlow>
      <responseFlow>
         <handler type="receiver"/>
      </responseFlow>
   </service>
   <transport name="http"
      pivot="java:org.apache.axis.transport.http.HTTPSender"/>
</deployment>
```

Why not sign and then encrypt? If you do it this way, then resulting message will be like:

```
<Header>
   <Security>
      <EncryptedKey>...</EncryptedKey>
      <Signature>...digest of the body element...</Signature>
   </Security>
</Header>
<Body>
   encrypted data...
</Body>
```

Problem! People may guess what is the original body element, calculate its digest and compare to this one.

On the other hand, if you encrypt it first and then sign it, it will be like:

People may try to guess the original body element and encrypt it (using the public of SecureService) and then calculate its digest. However, during encryption a random element is introduced, so the results of two encryptions will be different, so this won't work.

```
<Header>
   <Security>
      <Signature>...digest of the encrypted body element...</Signature>
      <EncryptedKey>...</EncryptedKey>
   </Security>
</Header>
<Body>
   encrypted data...
</Body>
```

Now the client is done. For the service, modify deploy.wsdd:

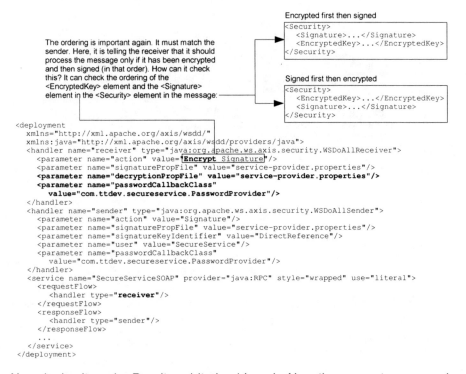

The ordering is important again. It must match the sender. Here, it is telling the receiver that it should process the message only if it has been encrypted and then signed (in that order). How can it check this? It can check the ordering of the <EncryptedKey> element and the <Signature> element in the <Security> element in the message:

Encrypted first then signed
```
<Security>
  <Signature>...</Signature>
  <EncryptedKey>...</EncryptedKey>
</Security>
```

Signed first then encrypted
```
<Security>
  <EncryptedKey>...</EncryptedKey>
  <Signature>...</Signature>
</Security>
```

```
<deployment
  xmlns="http://xml.apache.org/axis/wsdd/"
  xmlns:java="http://xml.apache.org/axis/wsdd/providers/java">
  <handler name="receiver" type="java:org.apache.ws.axis.security.WSDoAllReceiver">
    <parameter name="action" value="Encrypt Signature"/>
    <parameter name="signaturePropFile" value="service-provider.properties"/>
    <parameter name="decryptionPropFile" value="service-provider.properties"/>
    <parameter name="passwordCallbackClass"
      value="com.ttdev.secureservice.PasswordProvider"/>
  </handler>
  <handler name="sender" type="java:org.apache.ws.axis.security.WSDoAllSender">
    <parameter name="action" value="Signature"/>
    <parameter name="signaturePropFile" value="service-provider.properties"/>
    <parameter name="signatureKeyIdentifier" value="DirectReference"/>
    <parameter name="user" value="SecureService"/>
    <parameter name="passwordCallbackClass"
      value="com.ttdev.secureservice.PasswordProvider"/>
  </handler>
  <service name="SecureServiceSOAP" provider="java:RPC" style="wrapped" use="literal">
    <requestFlow>
      <handler type="receiver"/>
    </requestFlow>
    <responseFlow>
      <handler type="sender"/>
    </responseFlow>
    ...
  </service>
</deployment>
```

Now deploy it again. Run it and it should work. Now the request message is encrypted and signed, but the response message is only signed. To encrypt it, modify deploy.wsdd:

```
<deployment
  xmlns="http://xml.apache.org/axis/wsdd/"
  xmlns:java="http://xml.apache.org/axis/wsdd/providers/java">
  <handler name="receiver"
    type="java:org.apache.ws.axis.security.WSDoAllReceiver">
    <parameter name="action" value="Encrypt Signature"/>
    <parameter name="signaturePropFile" value="service-provider.properties"/>
    <parameter name="decryptionPropFile" value="service-provider.properties"/>
    <parameter name="passwordCallbackClass"
      value="com.ttdev.secureservice.PasswordProvider"/>
  </handler>
  <handler name="sender" type="java:org.apache.ws.axis.security.WSDoAllSender">
    <parameter name="action" value="Encrypt Signature"/>
    <parameter name="signaturePropFile" value="service-provider.properties"/>
    <parameter name="signatureKeyIdentifier" value="DirectReference"/>
    <parameter name="user" value="SecureService"/>
    <parameter name="passwordCallbackClass"
      value="com.ttdev.secureservice.PasswordProvider"/>
    <parameter name="encryptionPropFile" value="service-provider.properties"/>
    <parameter name="encryptionUser" value="john"/>
    <parameter name="encryptionKeyIdentifier" value="DirectReference"/>
  </handler>
  <service name="SecureServiceSOAP" provider="java:RPC"
    style="wrapped" use="literal">
    <requestFlow>
      <handler type="receiver"/>
    </requestFlow>
    <responseFlow>
```

```
      <handler type="sender"/>
    </responseFlow>
    ...
  </service>
</deployment>
```

Deploy it again. As it needs to have John's certificate, import it:

```
c:\keys>keytool -import -alias john -keystore service.ks -file john.cer
Enter keystore password:  service-ks-pass
Certificate was added to keystore
```

However, the change of the keystore won't take effect because it is cached by the WSS4J handlers. For it to take effect, you need to reload the web application. On the client, modify client-config.wsdd:

```
<deployment
  xmlns="http://xml.apache.org/axis/wsdd/"
  xmlns:java="http://xml.apache.org/axis/wsdd/providers/java">
  <handler name="sender" type="java:org.apache.ws.axis.security.WSDoAllSender">
    <parameter name="action" value="Encrypt Signature"/>
    <parameter name="signaturePropFile" value="client-provider.properties"/>
    <parameter name="signatureKeyIdentifier" value="DirectReference"/>
    <parameter name="user" value="john"/>
    <parameter name="passwordCallbackClass"
      value="com.ttdev.secureservice.client.PasswordPrompter"/>
    <parameter name="encryptionPropFile" value="client-provider.properties"/>
    <parameter name="encryptionUser" value="SecureService"/>
    <parameter name="encryptionKeyIdentifier" value="DirectReference"/>
  </handler>
  <handler name="receiver"
    type="java:org.apache.ws.axis.security.WSDoAllReceiver">
    <parameter name="action" value="Encrypt Signature"/>
    <parameter name="signaturePropFile" value="client-provider.properties"/>
    <parameter name="decryptionPropFile" value="client-provider.properties"/>
    <parameter name="passwordCallbackClass"
      value="com.ttdev.secureservice.client.PasswordProvider"/>
  </handler>
  <service name="SecureServiceSOAP">
    <requestFlow>
      <handler type="sender"/>
    </requestFlow>
    <responseFlow>
      <handler type="receiver"/>
    </responseFlow>
  </service>
  <transport name="http"
    pivot="java:org.apache.axis.transport.http.HTTPSender"/>
</deployment>
```

Note that it is using the PasswordProvider instead of the PasswordPrompter. It just doesn't make much sense to prompt the user in order to decrypt incoming messages. Now run it and it should work. You can confirm that the response is indeed encrypted and signed using the TCP Monitor.

Interoperability

If you're going to sign or encrypt SOAP messages, you need to check if the other side supports the WS-Security standard. If yes, you should further check what cryptographic algorithms are supported. Here are the algorithms supported by WSS4J:

Purpose	Supported algorithms
Digital signature	SHA1RSA

Purpose	Supported algorithms
Symmetric encryption	3DES, AES128, AES192, AES256
Encrypting the symmetric key ("key transport algorithm")	RSA15

You can tell WSS4J what algorithms to use by setting properties:

```
<parameter name="signatureAlgorithm" value="SHA1RSA"/>
<parameter name="encryptionSymAlgorithm" value="AES256"/>
<parameter name="encryptionKeyTransportAlgorithm" value="RSA15"/>
```

Summary

You can install a request handler and a response handler surrounding a client or your back end service object. They can perform functions without you changing your client or service code. To install a handler on the client side, you can do it in code or in the client-config.wsdd file. The latter is probably better because it works with both DII clients and clients using a stub. To do it on the server side, this is done in the WSDD file for the service.

To communicate with a handler, typically you set properties in the message context or the Call object. The message context will automatically get a copy of the properties of the Call object. If you're using a stub and thus don't have access to the Call object, you can call set the properties on the stub and it will pass them to the Call object automatically. If the handler has something to tell you, it will also use properties to tell you.

To sign a request message, install a do all sender from WSS4J as a request handler on the client. You need to set the action of the sender to "Signature", set the alias to use, the password callback class and a provider properties file. The provider properties file specifies what cryptographic provider to use (e.g., JDK), the location of the keystore and the keystore password. To verify the signature, you need to install a do all receiver from WSS4J for the service. You need to set the action to "Signature" so that it processes the message only if it has been signed. You also need to set the provider properties file. After verification, it will store the result in a property in the message context for your back end object to use. You may then perform further authorization based on the DN stored there.

To encrypt a request message, for the client side handler, set the action to "Encrypt" and set the alias to use and the provider properties file. To decrypt it, for the server side handler, set the action to "Encrypt" so that it processes the message only if it has been encrypted. You also need to set the password callback class and the provider properties file.

To configure the do all sender to both sign and encrypt, you should encrypt first and then sign for better security. On the receiver, make sure the action matches exactly that of the sender.

You can configure the sender to include the whole certificate or just the issuer DN plus the serial number in the message. If you're sure the receiver should have the required certificate, then it's more efficient to just send the issuer DN plus the serial number. Otherwise you will have to send the whole certificate.

Your password callback handler may prompt the user for the password, query a database, read a smart card and etc. It may make sense to pass the context information to it so that it can justify its action. To do that, use properties.

Chapter 10

Securing an Axis installation

What's in this chapter?

In this chapter you'll learn how to secure an Axis installation.

Removing unnecessary servlets

First, let's copy the SimpleService project and paste it as SecureAxis. Then open the context/WEB-INF/web.xml file in the project. You will inspect the stuff in there and remove anything that is unnecessary:

Continue with the rest of the web.xml file:

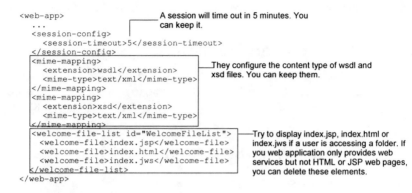

So, the cleaned up web.xml should be like:

```
<web-app>
  <display-name>Apache-Axis</display-name>
  <listener>
    <listener-class>
      org.apache.axis.transport.http.AxisHTTPSessionListener
    </listener-class>
  </listener>
  <servlet>
    <servlet-name>AxisServlet</servlet-name>
    <display-name>Apache-Axis Servlet</display-name>
    <servlet-class>org.apache.axis.transport.http.AxisServlet</servlet-class>
  </servlet>
  <servlet-mapping>
    <servlet-name>AxisServlet</servlet-name>
    <url-pattern>/servlet/AxisServlet</url-pattern>
  </servlet-mapping>
  <servlet-mapping>
    <servlet-name>AxisServlet</servlet-name>
    <url-pattern>/services/*</url-pattern>
  </servlet-mapping>
  <session-config>
    <session-timeout>5</session-timeout>
  </session-config>
  <mime-mapping>
    <extension>wsdl</extension>
    <mime-type>text/xml</mime-type>
  </mime-mapping>
  <mime-mapping>
    <extension>xsd</extension>
    <mime-type>text/xml</mime-type>
  </mime-mapping>
</web-app>
```

Create a context descriptor SecureAxis.xml for it. Modify build.xml:

```
<project name="SimpleService">
  ...
  <target name="deploy">
    <axis-admin
      url="http://localhost:8080/SecureAxis/servlet/AxisServlet"
      xmlfile="com/ttdev/simpleservice/deploy.wsdd"/>
  </target>
  <target name="undeploy">
    <axis-admin
      url="http://localhost:8080/SecureAxis/servlet/AxisServlet"
      xmlfile="com/ttdev/simpleservice/undeploy.wsdd"/>
  </target>
</project>
```

Deploy it the service. You should still be able to access the web service, e.g., using http://localhost:8080/SecureAxis/services/SimpleServiceSOAP?wsdl.

Disabling the web service listing

In addition to allowing people to deploy services, the Axis servlet can also list the services installed. For example, try to access http://localhost:8080/SecureAxis/servlet/AxisServlet in a browser and you'll see:

This is bad for security. To disable this listing function, modify web.xml:

```
<web-app>
  ...
  <servlet>
    <servlet-name>AxisServlet</servlet-name>
    <display-name>Apache-Axis Servlet</display-name>
    <servlet-class>org.apache.axis.transport.http.AxisServlet</servlet-class>
    <init-param>
      <param-name>axis.disableServiceList</param-name>
      <param-value>1</param-value>
    </init-param>
  </servlet>
  ...
</web-app>
```

Reload the application so that the changes take effect. Then try to list the services again and this time it won't work.

Axis HTTP Servlet

Hi, you have reached the AXIS HTTP Servlet.
Normally you would be hitting this URL with a
SOAP client rather than a browser.

In case you are interested, my AXIS transport
name appears to be 'http'

Removing the Version web service

From the service listing you can see that there are two services not defined by you:

The AdminService is called by the Axis servlet to deploy your services and thus needs to be there. The Version service will tell people what is the version of Axis that is running. This is bad for security. To remove it, you need to know where they were defined. Check the context/WEB-INF/server-config.wsdd file:

```
<deployment ...>
  ...
  <service name="SimpleServiceSOAP" ...>
    ...
  </service>
  <service name="AdminService" provider="java:MSG">
    <parameter name="allowedMethods" value="AdminService"/>
    <parameter name="enableRemoteAdmin" value="false"/>
    <parameter name="className" value="org.apache.axis.utils.Admin"/>
    <namespace>http://xml.apache.org/axis/wsdd/</namespace>
  </service>
  <service name="Version" provider="java:RPC">
    <parameter name="allowedMethods" value="getVersion"/>
    <parameter name="className" value="org.apache.axis.Version"/>
  </service>
  ...
</deployment>
```

How they got there? Both the Admin service and the Version service are defined by the default Axis server configuration, so they are copied into there automatically. To remove the Version service, remove it from the file and then reload the web application. To check if it has been removed, try to access http://localhost:8080/SecureAxis/services/Version?wsdl and it should tell you it can't find the service:

Restricting who can deploy services

Finally, the most important issue: How to prevent other people from deploying services to your Axis server? If you just disable the Admin service, then even you can't deploy services to it. To solve the problem, you can enforce that only

certain users can call the Admin service but not others. To do that, modify the
server-config.wsdd file:

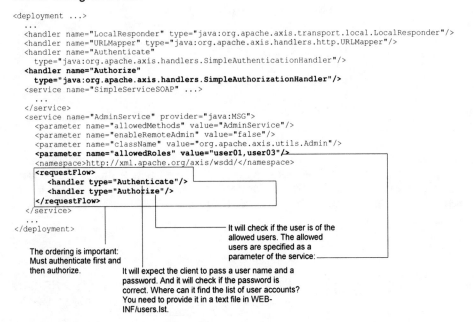

```
<deployment ...>
  ...
  <handler name="LocalResponder" type="java:org.apache.axis.transport.local.LocalResponder"/>
  <handler name="URLMapper" type="java:org.apache.axis.handlers.http.URLMapper"/>
  <handler name="Authenticate"
    type="java:org.apache.axis.handlers.SimpleAuthenticationHandler"/>
  <handler name="Authorize"
    type="java:org.apache.axis.handlers.SimpleAuthorizationHandler"/>
  <service name="SimpleServiceSOAP" ...>
    ...
  </service>
  <service name="AdminService" provider="java:MSG">
    <parameter name="allowedMethods" value="AdminService"/>
    <parameter name="enableRemoteAdmin" value="false"/>
    <parameter name="className" value="org.apache.axis.utils.Admin"/>
    <parameter name="allowedRoles" value="user01,user03"/>
    <namespace>http://xml.apache.org/axis/wsdd/</namespace>
    <requestFlow>
      <handler type="Authenticate"/>
      <handler type="Authorize"/>
    </requestFlow>
  </service>
  ...
</deployment>
```

The ordering is important:
Must authenticate first and
then authorize.

It will expect the client to pass a user name and a
password. And it will check if the password is
correct. Where can it find the list of user accounts?
You need to provide it in a text file in WEB-
INF/users.lst.

It will check if the user is of the
allowed users. The allowed
users are specified as a
parameter of the service:

Create the WEB-INF/users.lst file:

```
user01 pass01
user02 pass02
user03 pass03
```

Reload the web application for the changes to take effect. Now, try to run
deploy the service to see if you can still deploy it. It should fail because you're
not specifying a user name and password:

```
Console ×    Properties  Search
<terminated> SecureAxis build.xml [Ant Build] C:\Program Files\Java\jre1.5.0_02\bin\javaw.exe (Jan 1, 2006 6:43:49 PM)
Buildfile: C:\workspace\SecureAxis\build.xml
deploy:
[axis-admin] Processing file C:\workspace\SecureAxis\com\ttdev\simpleservice\deploy.w
[axis-admin] AxisFault
[axis-admin] faultCode: {http://xml.apache.org/axis/}HTTP
[axis-admin] faultSubcode:
[axis-admin] faultString: (401)Unauthorized
```

Now, try to connect as user01:

```
<project name="SimpleService">
  ...
  <target name="deploy">
    <axis-admin
      username="user01"
      password="pass01"
      url="http://localhost:8080/SecureAxis/servlet/AxisServlet"
      xmlfile="com/ttdev/simpleservice/deploy.wsdd"/>
  </target>
  <target name="undeploy">
    <axis-admin
```

```
          username="user01"
          password="pass01"
          url="http://localhost:8080/SecureAxis/servlet/AxisServlet"
          xmlfile="com/ttdev/simpleservice/undeploy.wsdd"/>
    </target>
  </project>
```
Run it again and it should work.

Removing the JWS handler

Let's check the server-config.wsdd file again:

```
<deployment ...>
  <globalConfiguration>
    <parameter name="sendMultiRefs" value="true"/>
    <parameter name="disablePrettyXML" value="true"/>
    <parameter name="adminPassword" value="admin"/>
    <parameter name="attachments.Directory"
      value="C:\workspace\SimpleService\context\WEB-INF\attachments"/>
    <parameter name="dotNetSoapEncFix" value="true"/>
    <parameter name="enableNamespacePrefixOptimization" value="false"/>
    <parameter name="sendXMLDeclaration" value="true"/>
    <parameter name="attachments.implementation"
      value="org.apache.axis.attachments.AttachmentsImpl"/>
    <parameter name="sendXsiTypes" value="true"/>
    <requestFlow>
      <handler type="java:org.apache.axis.handlers.JWSHandler">
        <parameter name="scope" value="session"/>
      </handler>
      <handler type="java:org.apache.axis.handlers.JWSHandler">
        <parameter name="scope" value="request"/>
        <parameter name="extension" value=".jwr"/>
      </handler>
    </requestFlow>
  </globalConfiguration>
  ...
</deployment>
```

Two instances of the JWS handler are installed in the global request flow. It means no matter what service this request is calling, it will go through these handlers. This handler is used to compile .jws files into .class files.

As you don't need this function, you can delete the <requestFlow> element. Reload the web application and it should continue to work.

Summary

For security, you should disable the unnecessary servlets, services and handlers. For servlets, check the WEB-INF/web.xml file. For services and handlers, check the WEB-INF/server-config.wsdd file.

For the Admin service which must be enabled, you should make sure only authorized users can call it to deploy services. To do that, install a simple authentication handler and a simple authorization handler for that service. You can define the users in WEB-INF/users.lst. The allowed users are set as a parameter for the service.

References

- Axis developers. Axis Documentation. http://ws.apache.org/axis/java/index.html.

- Jay Paulsen. Web app using log4j not garbage collected when shutdown with tomcat manager app. http://marc.theaimsgroup.com/?l=log4j-user&m=109585712427674&w=2.

- OASIS. Web Services Security: 3 SOAP Message Security 1.0 (WS-Security 2004). http://docs.oasis-open.org/wss/2004/01/oasis-200401-wss-soap-message-security-1.0.

- OASIS. Web Services Security UsernameToken Profile 1.0. http://docs.oasis-open.org/wss/2004/01/oasis-200401-wss-username-token-profile-1.0.

- OASIS. Web Services Security X.509 Certificate Token Profile. http://docs.oasis-open.org/wss/2004/01/oasis-200401-wss-x509-token-profile-1.0.

- Patrick Peak. Your Web App is leaking memory during restarts - Here's why...http://www.patrickpeak.com/page/patrick/20050614#your_web_app_is_leaking.

- Russell Butek. Web services programming tips and tricks: SOAP attachments with JAX-RPC. http://www-128.ibm.com/developerworks/webservices/library/ws-tip-soapjax.html.

- Russell Butek. Which style of WSDL should I use? http://www-128.ibm.com/developerworks/webservices/library/ws-whichwsdl/?ca=dgr-devx-WebServicesMVP03.

- Sang Shin. Secure Web services. http://www.javaworld.com/javaworld/jw-03-2003/jw-0321-wssecurity.html.

- Sun Microsystems. Java™ API for XML-based RPC (JAX-RPC 1.1). http://jcp.org/jsr/detail/101.jsp.

- Tomcat developers. Tomcat Documentation. http://jakarta.apache.org/tomcat.

- W3C. Namespaces in XML. http://www.w3.org/TR/1999/REC-xml-names-19990114.

- W3C. Simple Object Access Protocol (SOAP) 1.1. http://www.w3.org/TR/2000/NOTE-SOAP-20000508.

- W3C. SOAP Messages with Attachments. http://www.w3.org/TR/2000/NOTE-SOAP-attachments-20001211.

- W3C. URIs, URLs, and URNs: Clarifications and Recommendations 1.0. http://www.w3.org/TR/2001/NOTE-uri-clarification-20010921.

- W3C. Web Services Description Language (WSDL) 1.1. http://www.w3.org/TR/2001/NOTE-wsdl-20010315.

- W3C. XML Encryption Syntax and Processing. http://www.w3.org/TR/2002/REC-xmlenc-core-20021210.

- W3C. XML Schema Part 0: Primer Second Edition. http://www.w3.org/TR/2004/REC-xmlschema-0-20041028.

- W3C. XML Schema Part 1: Structures Second Edition. http://www.w3.org/TR/2004/REC-xmlschema-1-20041028.

- W3C. XML Schema Part 2: Datatypes Second Edition. http://www.w3.org/TR/2004/REC-xmlschema-2-20041028.

- W3C. XML-Signature Syntax and Processing. http://www.w3.org/TR/2002/REC-xmldsig-core-20020212.

- Will Provost. WSDL First. http://webservices.xml.com/pub/a/ws/2003/07/22/wsdlfirst.html.

- WS-I. WS-I Basic Profile Version 1.0. http://www.ws-i.org/Profiles/BasicProfile-1.0-2004-04-16.html.

- WSS4J developers. WSS4J Axis Deployment Tutorial. http://ws.apache.org/wss4j/axis.html.

Alphabetical Index

.NET..
    Interoperability..88
    Interoperability regarding attachments..105
<EncryptedData>..134
<EncryptedKey>..150
<Fault>..94
<Security>..134
Admin servlet..160
Asymmetric encryption..115
Authentication handler..164
Authorization handler..164
Axis..
    Installing...26
Axis client...
    How a message flows through...140
    Performing configurations at deployment time............................139
    Request handler..131
    Response flow...147
    Response handler...131, 145
    Setting the port name..143
    Transport...140
Axis server..
    Request handler..136
    Response flow...146
    Response handler..145
    Setting up...28
Axis servlet..55, 160
Binding..17
Bouncy castle...151
Build.xml..48
CA..118
Call object..72
    Setting properties of..138
Callback..132
CallbackHandler...132
Certificate...118
Certificate authority..118
Certificate chain...129
Certificate path...129
Client stub..58
Client-config.wsdd..141
CN..119
Configuring Java to use a proxy...75
Context descriptor..28

Context path..28
Cryptographic provider...133
  Merlin...133
DataHandler...104
Debugging a web service...67
Default constructor...79
Deploying a web service...53
Deserialization..78
Digital signature..117
DII..72
DIME...105
Disabling the web service listing..162
Distinguished name..119
DN..119
Document style..14
DOM..72
DSA...122
Dynamic Invocation Interface...72
Eclipse...26
Encoded..98
Encrypting a message...148
Encryption key...119
Endpoint..10
Endpoint provided by Axis...33
Fault...94
Getting the wsdl of a web serivce...58
How the session is maintained..111
IANA...21
Identifying the certificate used..134
    Embedding the certificate...135
    Using the issuer and serial number..134
Input message...12
International Assigned Numbers Association...................................21
Interoperability...
    Regarding attachments...105
    Regarding WS-Security...155
    With .NET..88
Java bean..79
JavaBeans Activation Framework..26
Jws support...160
Keystore..121
  Alias...121
  Alias password...122
  Generating a certificate request..124
  Generating a key pair...121
  Importing a certificate..127
  Password..122
Keytool..121

Listing the web services..57
Literal...34, 98
Local name...11
MD5...122
Message digest...116
MessageContext..138
MIME...105
MustUnderstand...
   Setting to false..135
Namespace...10
Namespace prefix..12
One way hash..116
OpenSSL..124
Operation...10
Part..12
Performance..
   By coarse grained interfaces...94
PKI..119
Port..18
Port type..16
Private key...114
Public key..114
Public key infrastructure...119
QName...11
Qualified name..11
Remote Procedure Call..13
Removing the JWS handler..165
Removing the Version web service..162
Removing unnecessary servlets...160
Restricting who can deploy services...163
RPC provider...53
RPC style...13
RSA...122
Schema...12
   Target namespace...13
Scope of service object..
   Application scope..109
   Request scope..109
   Session scope..110
Seeing the SOAP messages...73
Serialization..78
Serializer..78
Serializer factory...78
Server-config.wsdd..56
Service stub..48
Servlet...55
ServletContextListener..151
Setting the endpoint in the client..66

Setting up a CA..124
SHA1...122
Signing...117
Signing a message...129
Signing and then encrypting...152
Simple Object Access Protocol..17
SOAP...17
SOAP body element..34
SOAP envelope...34
SOAP header element..34
SOAP header entry...
     MustUnderstand...134
SOAP message format...34
SOAP monitor servlet...160
SOAP with Attachments..102
Symmetric encryption...114
TCP Monitor..73
Tomcat..26
     Manager..52
     Reloading an application..53
Type mapping..78
Type mapping registry..78
Undeploying a web service..61
Uniform Resource Identifier...21
Uniform Resource Name...21
URI...21
URL...21
URN...21
     Namespace identifier..21
     Namespace specific string...21
     NID..21
     NSS...21
Verifying a digital signature...136
Web application...
     Folder structure of...64
     Listener..151
     Reloading automatically...66
     Removing dangling references to resources...............................151
Web service..10
Web Service Deployment Descriptor...53
Web Services Description Language)...22
Web tools platform..31
Wrapped convention...86
Wrapped style..53
WS-I...15
WS-Security...155
WSDD...53
WSDL..22, 33

Target namespace..33
WSDL2Java..48
    Controlling how to map namespaces to packages.....................50
WSS4J...129
    Do all receiver...136
    Do all sender...131
    How it stores the results...144
    WSHandlerResult..144
    WSSecurityEngineResult..144
WTP...31
XML schema...
    Attributes..90
    MaxOccurs..90
    MinOccurs...90
Xsd..14
Xsi...14

Printed in the United States
100163LV00004B/274-276/A